YOU CAN'T HAVE MY MONEY!

A 6-STEP GUIDE TO GROW TAX-FREE WEALTH AND
RETIREMENT INCOME BY SMART INVESTING IN
AFTER-TAX ACCOUNTS, ACTIVE-MANAGED FUNDS,
AND CASH-VALUE LIFE INSURANCE

PAXTON S. FINNEGAN

CONTENTS

A Special Gift

As a token of my appreciation, I'd like to offer you a free online copy of *The Law-Abiding Pirate,* my guide to further secure your money against the ravages of inflation through the fledgling world of cryptocurrency, and the ancient art of treasure hunting for gold, silver, and other precious metals! Follow the link below to my website to let us know the email address where you would like your gift to be sent. Enjoy!

www.paxtonsfinnegan.com

(PS: Yes, that might be a pen name. Either that or my parents wanted everyone to think that I was named after a famed Confederate General from the Civil War.)

INTRODUCTION

When you grow up on a ranch, getting trampled by cows on a semi-regular basis, you tend to develop a passive attitude toward the rest of the goings-on of your everyday life. Sure, times may be tough at the moment. But I'm not getting trampled by a cow, so it's not so bad. That's just how life is.

However, I quickly learned that this is a bad attitude to adapt when it comes to finances. While focusing on the various ways in which "It could be worse" in any given scenario will help us to appreciate the blessings in our lives, it does run the risk of developing an apathetic outlook on future planning. For the longest time, I thought I'd save enough for a comfortable retirement just by doing things "the way we've always done it": Get a job. Work hard. Buy a house. Save when you can. Have a nest egg for retirement.

And suddenly I was in my mid-30s, trying to think if I'd ever once had $10,000 sitting in a basic bank account. A few quick calculations on a napkin told me that I needed new ways of both growing my income and planning for my retirement.

The problem is that, although we all want to make the best decisions we can for ourselves, there's a lot of important things to know that just don't get covered in the classroom. We end up learning our financial skills from our peers, and our families. We can learn a lot of wise sayings about saving from family but it takes more than just budgeting some monthly cash into a savings account to feel secure when your hair starts turning grey. Especially when times get tough, and the budget we've carefully built starts getting ornery.

It's the nature of the beast for money matters to get tricky, but it's also in the nature of the community to share our skills so we can all learn from one another. This book is here to help you take steps towards setting up a solid life for yourself before you reach the end of your career, as well as making plans for the security of your family.

Education doesn't matter. I'll be a blue-collar grunt till the day I die, God willing. Income level, while something we all strive to improve, doesn't matter as much as we think it does. Even with a small monthly amount budgeted towards smart investments, we can build a confident future.

We can be in middle-management, hitting it hard from nine to five. We can be that teenager working our first job, flipping hamburgers. Or we could be a grey-haired Granny wondering if our lifetime of work will tide us over to our final resting place. It doesn't matter where on the spectrum we fall. There are all kinds of seminars and books teaching people a new way to get rich, or the perfect stocks and innovations to invest in, and I do not question the validity of any of them: Many people following them have achieved great success, while others have failed. That's just not what I'm interested in. I'm interested in a road-map that can be followed by anyone, regardless of our income level, to maximize the potential growth and savings of whatever money we have. I've worked with a lot of impoverished people in my lifetime, some self-afflicted, and others failed by a lack of basic financial methodology in school. I want to help them get on a better course, even while working a minimum-wage or part-time job. And, even if we have been blessed with the highest levels of education and a great income, this book can help us solidify those earnings into a rock-solid retirement.

Because we've all seen entire industries collapse overnight, and the richest among us lose everything. We need more than income. We need an underpinning financial plan to anchor us through tumultuous times, keeping us on a course toward success.

If done right, our job becomes the least important part of the process.

We'll learn about when our bank is our best friend, and when we're better off remembering that they're a business first. We'll learn how to best utilize our existing debts, and how even debt can play a huge role in enabling us to maximize our long-term investments. We'll learn about exciting new strategies for growing investments through things as basic as our mortgages and life insurance coverage. And, above all, we'll learn how to keep our lifelong earnings from being gouged by the omnipresent tax-man at the end of the day.

I can't speak for the entire world's economic system. Every national government will have an entirely different financial and banking system and different levels of economic opportunity for the ground-level working folks. Even in the United States, a lot of investment opportunities will vary greatly from state to state. However, what I did notice over several years of research was the strong parallels in financial opportunities and economic strategies across North America. These have enabled some free trade opportunities which the rest of the world would normally find difficult, seen first in NAFTA and later in the USMCA. International transactions have never been easier, business people frequently work on both sides of borders, and even basic banking needs and investment products have borrowed freely from one another. This more strongly aligns daily strategies which the average person can use, regardless of what country they live in. For that reason, I've tried to incorporate investment variations that will be useful to over 300 million American readers, as well as to their almost 40 million northern neighbors in Canada. While the names and specific details of some products may vary by region, I will try to group similar tools for ease of understanding, or discuss ways to implement methods not fully available in our area yet.

Even if every specific option is not available to our state or province, the trend has been that something else very similar may be available if we do a little digging, or the strategies which have been most successful in one nation can be readily adapted for use in another. Find the one that appeals most strongly to you, regardless of its country of origin, and see how easily it can be implemented into your daily financial strategy. Strengthening the financial foundations of everyday citizens in allied nations leads both countries to stronger trade agreements, more widely available investment products, and a truly enviable international relationship.

Fair warning: You'll hear me sing the praises of Capitalistic freedom and Judeo-Christian values in this book, and make jokes about the Commies and blue-haired people. Just in case my approval of international banking parallels was leading any of you to believe that I have globalist sympathies. Nope. Throughout history, the world has functioned most efficiently and thrived most financially when nations embraced and balanced personal freedoms, financial opportunity, and military strength. Freely borrowing, analyzing, and adapting international ideas is a major key to the prosperity of any sovereign state, but keep a watch set on the gates.

Seriously, the title of this book is *You Can't Have My Money!* Did you think you were going to find that Socialism blueprint hyped by your blue-haired Gender Studies professor in here?

1

WE DON'T ALL DIE FROM BLACK LUNG AT AGE 45 ANYMORE:

HOW VACCINES, ADVANCES IN TECHNOLOGY, HIGHER STANDARDS OF LIVING, AND A BUNCH OF LONELY SOLDIERS COMING HOME FROM STOMPING ON NAZIS CHANGED THE WESTERN WORLD FOREVER.

Gather round, folks, and let's take a look back to the last century. The Greatest Generation set us up on a path to prosperity that no one else in history can boast of, but it's important to note a few things they overlooked, quite understandably at the time. Once we know these things, it becomes easy for us to correct their missteps to make the most of the unprecedented opportunities they afforded to us.

A New Life

September 1945: World War II had just ended, and the ramifications of this would be huge for low-wage, blue-collar workers throughout the North American continent.

Because the inefficacy of cavalry and bayonet charges had been made brutally clear in the corpse-filled no man's land between Gallipoli trenches in World War I, factories were now churning out tanks, planes, amphibious landing craft, and industrial vehicles. These incredible advances in land, air, and sea vehicles required concurrent advances in factory automation to assemble them. When peacetime finally arrived, a whole new industrial stage had been set, and nobody was ready to set-strike them after the curtain dropped and just go back to the horse and buggy. For the first time in history, automated factory-production jobs were the norm, and workers for them were in high demand, not just for the military, but for the average citizen.

Backing our growing production base would be the advent of nuclear power: Another World War II innovation of conflict-resolution that nobody was ready to put into the dust-bin of history after General Douglas MacArthur had his infamous "No BS" sit-down—and equally infamous "god-shattering" photo taken—with Emperor Hirohito of Japan. The greatest and most terrible innovation in the history of mankind was first adapted to civilian electrical generation in 1958. It was an era of unprecedented optimism, and people spoke of the inevitability of flying cars without sarcasm.

Soldiers who'd been putting off starting a family for years were now ready for their stateside hero's welcome, which, as it turned out, involved a lot more than just brass bands and parades. The population boomed, and birth rates rose at an incredible rate across the world. In the United States alone, 76 million babies were born during this period, with a total of 90 million born across North America in the 18 years between 1946 and 1964.

In the 20th century alone, the world population went from 1.7 billion to over 6 billion people. This number is made all the more shocking when we stop to consider the hundreds of millions who died within that same century as a result of two world wars and the genocidal rise of Communist regimes across the world in the aftermath.

More people being born, along with the peace and advances we already made, meant more people were reaching adulthood.

Because medical advances in vaccines, antibiotics, surgery, sterile medical storage, and hygiene made it easier to live longer, we got a far larger quantity of mature minds sharing great ideas. This led to still greater leaps forward in technology, lifestyle, and even workplace safety standards.

In the wake of the horrors of war was a renewed love for life, and that didn't just apply to the family setting. Hard hats, gloves, and steel-toed boots may seem like nothing special until you see the old black-and-white photos of construction crews building the Empire State Building without them. Men who had survived storming the beaches of Normandy were not exactly looking forward to coming home only to die in some cost-cutting mining operation, and they made dang sure that every employer in the USA knew it. Unions were rapidly formed to ensure fair treatment and pay for all workers, plus improved safety standards. After a few more years, the black-lunged coal miner carrying a pickax and a caged canary was suddenly operating an automated boring machine in a ventilated shaft with radon detectors and an emergency beacon on his belt.

More hands working together meant more hands to lay the wires and cables for infrastructure, funneling electricity and telephone reception into every home. Shortly thereafter, somebody invented this thing called the Internet.

As a result, the exchange of ideas would continue to compound itself.

Through all these advances, even the most impoverished nations saw an incredible rise in their overall wealth and life expectancy in less than a century of development. The amazing advances in health, technology, and professional practice fed back into itself, making it possible for larger amounts of people to live and succeed together, and then in turn support, and perhaps even become, the minds who'd think up the next wave of advances.

With fewer and fewer people needed to handle the now-automated necessities of survival like farming, construction, resource gathering, and energy production, even more have been freed to specialize in new areas of art, technology, and research. Gone are the days when a peasant farmer could produce enough grain to feed himself and three family members. One farmer with a tractor and combine harvester can now produce food for hundreds of people. All of this has led to even further development in increasingly esoteric fields of knowledge, full of serendipity to keep us propelling forward.

I have literally never used the word serendipity before, outside of referencing a pink sea dragon from a children's book. That just goes to show how deeply awed the past century has left me.

The Unexpected Mule in It All

But, of course, sometimes a stubborn mule manages to sneak among your selectively-bred champion Thoroughbreds. Despite the surge of innovation, one aspect of our day-to-day lives refused to budge, especially among those of us who aren't exactly ranked amongst the financial elite: We didn't know how to plan for retirement.

Ask a pioneer in the 1850s what his retirement plan was, and you'd probably get a blank stare and a demand to get your DeLorean off his silver claim. He planned to cut timbers, plant crops, milk cows, pan gold, and shoot game until he died of black lung at age 45. The dreams of "striking it rich" and "living like kings" were frequently spoken of, but rarely attained. Very often, there was no distinction between working years and sunset years: We worked right into the sunset and hoped that we didn't accidentally snuggle up under a smallpox blanket in the process. And we didn't mind, because work was just as much a part of a happy life as a family was.

It's also important to note that even the rare few who did find fortunes in previous centuries often didn't know how to manage their treasures, further evidence that we can learn new things all the time and still never learn from the past. The famous Canadian gold miner, William "Billy" Barker, first struck it rich in 1862, sifting an incredible 1/3 oz of gold per pan, and eventually pulling up gold nuggets by the bucketful from a 60-foot shaft. The resulting gold rush led to the creation of one of the most famous northern boomtowns, Barkerville, British Columbia, where gold-panning is still a popular tourist attraction today.

Billy Barker died penniless in 1894, and I doubt he was very happy about it.

Now, that's not to say that people nowadays aren't happy, or that we don't have a variety of tools and options for dealing with the retirement mule. For example, we have our typical High-Interest Savings Accounts (HISA) offered by most banks, generally offering annual returns of 1% to 1.5%. For those who want to feel secure in their sunset years, we also have our Individual Retirement Accounts (IRA), or its Canadian counterpart, the Registered Retirement Savings Plan (RRSP).

People looking to squeeze more productivity out of this mule have also been getting into the stock market or looking at mutual funds. Others think they'll be fine with only a workplace pension, and others do nothing more than drop all their spare change into a 4-gallon water jug on the kitchen counter for 50 years.

Even the white-collared professional can be stuck with surprisingly old-fashioned ideas, amongst other blind spots. Mistakes that happened in 1929 repeated in 2007 in the form of great market crashes, showing that, on some levels, things haven't changed much. Because of our long lives, we now have more time than ever to see ourselves make the same mistakes all over again. We need to find ways to avert that calamity, using the tools available to us. Unfortunately, we more often than not have to unearth these tools on our own. That's where this book can help us.

I Know I Won't Work as Well When I'm an Old Buzzard

When I was a 4-year-old kid, I would say, "*Waaah!* Why are the cookies always on the top shelf?!" Then, around the time I turned 40, I started saying, "*Gaaah! My back!* Why is everything always on the bottom shelf?!" Just because we're living longer doesn't mean we're necessarily able to work longer. We now have a prevalence of both junk food and sedentary jobs, ranging anywhere from office workers slumped over their computers to long-haul truck drivers. This means that a lot of our current aging population has nowhere near the vim and vigor of Grandpa Finnegan who died by chopping a mighty Redwood down on himself at age 93.

Despite rising life expectancy, most people still dislike the idea of working once we get into our sixties or seventies. Even before we reach that point, our relatively comfortable lives mean more and more people are aiming to retire at fifty or even forty, as higher quality of life makes it easier for us to push ourselves harder while we're young to enjoy a well-earned retirement early on.

However, regardless of how hard we work, or whether we retire at 40 or 70, we're going to need careful planning. Odds are, we're more than able to live into our 90s. The last thing we want is for our savings to dry up mid-retirement because we underestimated our longevity by a few decades.

Become the Nine

When I started to research and discuss with a few true financial wizards with whom I was blessed to be associated, I came across a simple phrase: 91 and 9. We're going to want to remember that one.

It means that 91% of people start their retirement fearful for their financial security. In a room of 1,000 people, 910 of them risk entering retirement unfulfilled, and with limited means to generate sufficient wealth using the time they have left. In the wake of the COVID-19 pandemic, some experts estimate that this number will rise as high as 97%. Other recent studies have shown that the number one fear of senior citizens is outliving their retirement funds, superseding even fears for their physical and mental health.

At the time of this writing, this problem of only 91% of people feeling comfortable about their retirement is consistent across North America, which is yet another reason that I felt it was important to cover strategies that could be utilized in both the USA and Canada: With numbers that bad, we need to look to the strategies being used on the other side of our border, for either direct copying or at least inspiration.

What we'll soon discover is that, despite some differences in terminology and financial products, the basic strategies work similarly well in both countries, and many could even be implemented in such diverse places as Australia, Mexico, the UK, or any other number of nations with a reasonable degree of economic freedom. The strategies parallel each other in many ways, so, no matter which country we live in, we can still find something that will get our money working harder for us.

This is one way to stumble across unexpected treasures. Sometimes, the economic norms practiced by our community, region, or even country simply don't work out as well as we'd hope. In these cases, it's the wise person who's able to look to their neighbor for help. Not in handouts, but in knowledge. With the shared knowledge of nations, it isn't just our next-door neighbor who we can feed for a lifetime by teaching him how to fish.

Even if it means pointing our financial telescope across state or provincial lines, or even if it means pointing that same scope across a sovereign state border, it's a good idea to seek inspiration from others. Especially when they're the ones succeeding.

However, we first need to take a look at some people who didn't succeed. Because there's a very good chance that we're doing the same thing they did.

2

THE YOUNG, EAGER, AND WOEFULLY UNPREPARED LIFE INSURANCE AGENT:

3 TALES OF HOW STICKING TO THE "HOW IT'S ALWAYS BEEN DONE" MENTALITY CAN LEAD TO FINANCIAL DISASTER.

S torytime!

Earlier, I mentioned just a couple of the ways that modern people prepare for their futures: HISAs, 401(k)s, and IRAs, or RRSPs for those in Canada. Then there are mutual funds, separate accounts, segregated funds, cash-value insurance products, Roth IRAs, and Tax-Free Savings Accounts.

Let's keep all of those in the back of our minds, as we'll be looking at each of them in-depth later on. Until then, let's look at...

Dan's Story

Dan is a police officer in his early 40s who lives in Denver, Colorado, with his wife and their four children. Given the high-risk nature of his job and the fact that he did not decide to serve his community until he was already in his early 30s, he decided to provide additional security for his family by purchasing a life insurance policy to be paid out to his family in the event of his untimely death.

Dan placed a call to a local agency and was offered a home visit to discuss his options. Two days later, he opened his front door to greet a young, well-dressed, and extremely eager life agent. After hearing the enthusiastic pitch, Dan wasn't fully certain of the details, but he was given every reassurance by his agent that the policy would be a perfect fit. Dan met all the qualifications, and the pre-authorized monthly payments were very reasonable. He signed for the policy. Dan now had a life insurance policy he was able to dutifully pay month after month, year after year. Or so he thought.

What neither he nor his agent realized was that no policy could sustain itself on the type of plan he had been offered. All policies need a certain amount paid to be viable. It's like a form of community donation: If the fund doesn't get enough paid in initially, then it won't have enough to help a person when they fall on hard times.

Almost ten years later, Dan was horrified to realize that his life insurance policy had been underfunded from the very beginning to the point where its cash value was only two years away from completely killing itself off. It is important to note that he had not been given notice from the insurance company regarding this underfunding. He had begun investigating on his own after a few years since something about his payment plan just didn't sound right to him.

When Dan realized how underfunded his policy was, he faced a stark choice: Pay up the staggering balance owing now to restore the full fund value, and henceforth pay increased premiums, or let the policy drop. He left messages with the agency, requesting a follow-up meeting to discuss other solutions. To this day, the agency has never returned his calls.

Dan had no choice but to cancel his policy with no hope of recovering any of the tens of thousands of dollars he had been paying for nearly a decade.

Having lost the feeling of security for his family's future, he had to start the long process of seeking out another, more credible company, with more knowledgeable agents to help guide him to a sustainable choice. He has since found relative success, but his earlier financial loss still hurts him. He treated a relatively new form of insurance the way his father or grandfather may have approached the life insurance policies of their generation, and he got burned for it.

Even as he's recovering, his plans for financial security have been set back by years.

Insurance policies aren't necessarily just "fire and forget" or "shoot and scoot." We can't always just set up a monthly payment to cover our premiums and be done with it. As interest rates and policy charges of a life insurance policy change, so must the amount that must be paid to keep the policy active.

For example, a common trait of some Universal Life Insurance policies is that, as a cost for its relative flexibility compared to other life insurance plans, we need to pay more as we age. Others will have an investment portion that accrues interest on our payments to keep the fund value high. But Dan had never been told that. He was told that as long as he paid what the agent said he should, then everything would be fine.

Stacy's Story

Stacy is a single mom from Chicago, Illinois, whose 14-year-old daughter Alana has a physical and learning disability. Whereas Dan often worried about what his family would do once he was gone, Stacy was more concerned with her daughter's future as a growing teen and future adult.

Going off the advice she had been raised with, Stacy decided to build up some cash through a mutual fund. Throughout her adult life, she had been told how hands-off and convenient they are, and how great they can be for building long-term wealth.

In simple terms, a mutual fund is when multiple investors pool part of their resources together and then give control over that pool to a team of finance managers and advisors. The management team smartly invests the fund to generate profit for all of the individual investors.

That's the theory at least, but we all know there can be a big difference between theory and actual practice.

Stacy was continually frustrated by what turned out to be a very passive management team with a grossly hands-off approach to investing,—the managers apparently believing that the "hands-off" description applied equally to all parties involved—and because she was only one small cog in the mutual fund, she found it very difficult to keep her participation in it aligned to her wants and needs. When it came to investment choice, there was not a lot of flexibility to be found in passive mutual funds.

All of that hassle, and she didn't even have the peace of mind in knowing that it was at least working. As it turned out, different parts of the fund would often suffer, and as a result, she would suffer. Her stress would mount as she became increasingly aware of how her investments would fall short of the returns she needed to help her daughter live the life she wanted.

Sadly, her management team wasn't just passive when it came to money, but also when it came to client support.

Anyone who's dealt with passive management in customer service knows that, when their system starts getting screwy like this, there's no one on hand to help you. At least, no one who works there. But at least you'll still get that customer satisfaction survey in your email within 15 minutes of slamming down the phone.

Taking matters into her own hands, Stacy tried to make up for the consistent losses of the fund by investing in other funds that are lower risk. Sadly, lower risk historically means lower returns, and this was the end result of her investments. She earned back a fraction of what she had planned and budgeted for.

While she managed to make ends meet, the way that single mothers always seem to do, giving her daughter that chance of a better life meant Stacy had to replan her entire retirement: The strategy change she was forced to make for the family to survive ultimately crippled their long-term finances. Stacy was left with no choice but to start structuring the rest of her life on a far more modest budget.

But what of the managers? What of the people who were supposed to be looking after the money she entrusted them with? A sad fact of life is that, whether a fund gains or loses money, the managers still get paid so long as the fund exists. They were never operating with her best interests in mind and had no real motivation to do so. In their minds, so what if one investor pulls out? They lost zero sleep, while Stacy was losing all of it.

Roy and Annie

Meanwhile, in Canada...

Roy and Annie are an elderly couple living in farm country outside of Edmonton, Alberta, who find themselves going through a disappointing retirement. People often say old habits die hard, and their old habit was spending decades listening to financial advice from their local bank.

A lot of the advice was good enough to build trust, trust which would become habitual credulity towards their bank tellers, but it turned out that Roy and Annie may have trusted too much. Either that or the bank assumed too much about this couple's knowledge of tax laws.

Regardless of whether trust or apathy was to blame, their bank failed to warn them about a key detail present in one of the services they were offering. For decades, the bank tellers were saying, over and over again, "Now is the best time to contribute to one of our offered RRSPs!" (Again for the sake of parallels, it is important to note that this same scenario regularly plays out in the case of elderly Americans who contributed a lifetime of payments to the RRSP's US counterpart, the traditional IRA.)

It seemed like a great decision at the time.

"RRSP income is exempt from tax while it remains in the plan," the bank teller assured them. "You can even deduct contributions from your annual income tax."

On the surface, this seemed like a great way for Roy and Annie to save their money for old age in a place that wouldn't be whittled away by taxes. Since all RRSPs are registered with the Canadian government, and since the government is usually interested in encouraging its citizens to save and plan for the long term, the plan seemed solid.

RRSP funds, like IRAs, are indeed tax-exempt while in the plan, but no one at the bank said anything to Roy and Annie about how that money would be taxed once withdrawn from the plan. Maybe these days we'll see a warning about this on official websites, but it's hardly written in bright red letters.

Imagine being in this couple's shoes. Roy and Annie made a home together, raised a family, and worked hard their whole lives. Whatever they earned, they spent carefully, budgeted well, and even invested wisely, seeing great gains for their future in compounding growth.

They did everything according to the accepted plan. By the time they were getting old and grey, they had squirreled away a respectable amount of money to ensure their wellbeing for the rest of their lives. Then retirement came, and they made their first withdrawal from their RRSP.

Only now, if Roy and Annie want $60, they need to take out $100.

The government never touched their RRSP while it was sitting tucked away and useless, but, as soon as that fund matured to the point of mandated withdrawals, Canada started helping itself to huge swathes of the money Roy and Annie were banking on for their everyday needs.

Ultimately, nearly 40% of what they withdrew had to go towards various back-end taxes. Fine print that not a single bank teller warned them about when encouraging them to sign up for an RRSP. Why? Because that particular RRSP was an investment product specific to their bank, so naturally it is the first thing their bank offered, as we'll discuss further in the next chapter.

Imagine saving up a specific amount for when we're no longer able to be effective in the workplace, only to be told at the last minute that we're only going to get slightly more than half of that back. We're well past our prime, and there's nothing we can do about it.

The older we get, the harder it becomes to bounce back. That's because we have far less recovery time before we need to worry about retiring and building up old-age security. And, in Canada, that's not just a generic phrase: Old Age Security, or OAS, is an additional payment made by the Canadian government to seniors citizens. However, portions of it can also be clawed back by the government based upon how much the individual has contributed to and withdrawn from their RRSP: The mandatory withdrawals are considered taxable income, and the amount of OAS a person is entitled to will be scaled according to their level of income.

The RRSPs that kept getting pitched to Roy and Annie by their small-town banker—who they knew better as "Sharon from church"—became their primary investment tool. They'd made the wrong choice of where to contribute the bulk of their investment money from day one because other options had never been discussed. Some had not even been invented yet, such as the Tax-Free Savings Account, or TFSA, which quietly arrived without Roy and Annie's knowledge in 2009. Not only were they never fully apprised of the limitations specific to their current investment tool, but they were never told the benefits of something new.

The Takeaway

We've just examined three key examples of what are considered to be staples for preparing our future and the futures of our family: Life insurance, mutual funds, and retirement accounts.

Just like Dan, Stacy, Roy, and Annie, we have likely been told that investing in any of those choices is just the rational and responsible thing to do. We've been told that it's not just rational and responsible, but also the *safe* thing to do. This is what I have seen friends, colleagues, and even mentors tell each other for decades. And bankers, of course.

However, we see here that none of those options are inherently safe, and, even if they are that generally means a lower return on our investments or a lower overall fund value. It's easy to hit a snag, even when we think we're being responsible. To meet a modern life's demands, it's not enough to just go with what people say we should do just because it looks like the most sensible choice. (I'll withhold my rant about the entirety of the Federal Reserve system for another book.)

It's important to look at each person's choice critically. Let's walk through how they could've done better for themselves, and what we can do differently if we ever find ourselves in their shoes.

The truth is, with the smallest of changes in strategy and approach, all of their stories could've been completely turned around. Many of their lives have started turning around for the better once they internalized the hard lessons they learned, and many others who were willing to listen to them found their own lives going much better for it. My own life included, as I could now look for alternatives to the choices they had made.

One story on its own won't always have all the answers, but once we collect more together, we begin realizing some remarkable things. Much of the advice below feeds into the strategies I'll be describing later on, but I'll also be covering some smaller common-sense stuff: Things we really ought to know, but don't usually get warned about when told to invest or insure ourselves in "the most responsible way."

Dan's Alternate Ending

The first thing Dan could've done was a little more research on his insurance company. Generally, the longer-lived and better-established a company is, the more certain we can be that it'll payout and remain strong throughout our lives, ready to lend us the aid we've been contributing to. Even if it costs a little more, we'll have the security of knowing that we're investing in a policy where the company knows what it's doing, and isn't just going to drop the ball when we need it.

However, beyond the hypothetical, Dan was dealing with a long-term, reputable agency, and not some scammer. So the next thing he could've done is take a little time to double-check everything the agent said, particularly regarding the actual operation and coverage of his specific policy. It's entirely possible that the young, eager life agent was simply inexperienced, and did not yet know how to build rapport and trust with his clients by explaining the policy in thorough, yet simplified, detail. A more thorough explanation of what was needed and what would be provided could have saved Dan a lot of grief.

No matter how sincere the agent is, there's a good chance that they don't know everything about what they're selling, especially when it comes to complex financial matters. As far as both Dan and the agent knew, they had worked out a deal where Dan was getting what he needed, with the agent probably knowing little more about Dan than his health status and annual income.

No one can fully know our circumstances, nor do most strangers care to. Not until a representative demonstrates a sincere desire to sit down and get to know us should we consider them as an option. This usually means finding an agent who plans on collecting information and conducting a full breakdown of our economic situation to come up with a detailed life plan. In short, they can't do that in one evening sitting around our kitchen table. If they show that they are willing to take a few extra days to come up with a customized solution for us, then that is the company we should probably be dealing with, as opposed to some young guy in a suit who constantly hears Alec Baldwin in his ear, muttering, "Always be closing."

It isn't always easy to think of the questions we need to ask in this situation, but it does demonstrate how important it is to get advice and speak to financially savvy people we can trust before we make big, life-changing decisions.

Stacy's Alternate Ending

It's easy to see how Stacy may have been bamboozled. She was often told that passive investment is historically the safer, more responsible long-term option. She had then heard that mutual funds are the ideal passive method to build extra income through initial investments, and countless people that she knew had been investing in them for years. When she heard this, she felt that they would only be passive in the sense that she wouldn't have to directly handle them. After all, that's what she was entrusting the mutual fund's professional finance team with in the first place.

Sadly, it turns out that 'passive' is kind of a loaded word in the world of mutual funds. "Passive is good" is the conventional wisdom, but passive mutual funds aren't the only way. Since she was already willing to pay a team to handle things for her, Stacy could've instead benefited from finding an active-managed fund instead. These are much more flexible in the sense that their professional managers actively monitor the accounts. They are willing and able to seize opportunities as they come by, or divert funds to a safer place when the market changes for the worse.

Active management means placing our money in the hands of people who will make bigger investments where repayment is most likely, and smaller investments where repayment is less likely while following the standard mutual fund method of dividing our investment into several different funds, generally in an 80/20 split based on our risk tolerance. The difference is in protective measures. For example, in a traditional mutual fund, if our 80% share suffers, we lose part of our investment, while our 20% share remains stable. However, an active manager has the entrusted ability to switch the market shares when things are not looking well: If our 80% share appears to be at risk of losing value, it can be switched with our 20% share, so the drop in our investment is minimized. The managers know to be that sensitive, even when choosing different bond options within a single company, and they're hands-on enough to be making those decisions constantly.

It's the exact opposite of the passive, "do it as we've always done it" way. If Stacy had combined this more active strategy with something like an active-managed mutual fund or segregated fund, she wouldn't just be smiling by now, she'd be laughing.

Roy and Annie's Alternate Ending

The knee-jerk response is to say that Roy and Annie should've ignored their bank teller's suggestions. Instead of putting almost all their eggs in one highly taxable basket, they could've diversified, and sought out other ways to contribute to their future, such as in (when it became available) a Tax-Free Savings Account—the Canadian equivalent of a Roth IRA.

Other strategies such as income-splitting could've also been used, but a good TFSA, perhaps operating within an actively managed investment fund, would have been the best way to minimize the clawback they experienced on their cash and OAS when they were finally withdrawing funds in retirement. Like the Roth IRA, there are no annual income tax deductions attached to contributions into the TFSA. However, once the full tax for that year is paid, the funds grow tax-free for the remainder of their investment period, so long as the annual contribution limit is not exceeded: The current limit as of this writing is $6,000 annually, so a simple contribution of $500 a month can safely grow our investment for as long as we like.

And, at the end of the day... when you take out $100, you get $100.

We will be taking a closer look at several different investment tools in the following chapters, which at first can seem a little complicated when we are dealing with different countries. Even in the US, some tools will differ slightly or at least have names that vary from state to state. However, it is noteworthy that many of the products were inspired by each other, although subsequently developed with slight variations in different nations or states. We will always be sure to emphasize which parallel product or strategy can be used, regardless of our region.

3

THAT'S HOW THEY GET YOU:

THE RED, FLASHING, EARDRUM-BURSTING WARNING BELLS WHEN YOUR BANK TRIES TO SELL YOU A MORTGAGE, MORTGAGE LIFE INSURANCE, AND HIGH-LIMIT CREDIT CARDS.

Although it can feel convenient to take advantage of every product our bank offers us, there's usually a better option out there. Figuring out what to do with that fact will be the first step in this book.

Step 1: Learn to Look Beyond Your Bank.

I have no problem with banks. For my part, I've been a steadfast customer to local banks, often for decades at a time, and they have come through for me in many difficult times. I have nothing but gratitude for the promotions they offered that ultimately saved me untold sums over the years.

All that being understood, it's still just a bank, and a bank is a business. They provide a service to us in exchange for a modest fee. It's not an exclusive relationship. Roy and Annie treated their bank too much like one,—after all, it was "Sharon from church"—and this is what stopped them from diversifying enough to truly be secure.

A bank won't feel insulted if we shop around before making our investments, but too many people only have one thought when it comes to managing their money: "Go to the bank!"

Most of us still put more confidence into something that's a little more brick-and-mortar than online investing or a faceless institution or product from out of state. People then justify not using anything else with feelings of community loyalty, which is just a home-town guilt trip. Openness to new financial options does not make one a "playa," or whatever it is that the kids are saying these days.

Banks are great at making money, but, let's be honest, most of them aren't so good at making *us* money. If they were equally good at both, they would've warned Roy and Annie about the back-end taxes during the RRSP pitch. Bankers thrive from bringing business to their specific institution. (Do you really believe that the maximization of a bank teller's Christmas bonus is contingent on how many IRAs they *didn't* sell that year?)

Keep banks on their toes. Keep them honest. Shop around, and let them know up-front that we are doing so. Sometimes that's all the motivation they need to find the best option for us.

What Can We Expect From Our Bank?

Although this might change soon, our bank should be offering what is considered to be a full range of accounts, including both traditional IRAs and Roth IRAs, the Roth generally being more interesting for readers of this book who are interested in minimizing our taxation in retirement. However, it's equally likely that all the accounts they offer are nothing more than savings accounts, which can be helpful but aren't the best quality choice for long-term investment. Normally, it's not a banker who'll help us find our ideal investment account, but a broker instead. We'll look more closely at brokers later on.

Besides general investment and retirement accounts, bankers will leap at every chance to offer three services: mortgages, mortgage life insurance, and high-limit credit cards. I accepted all three without question when I was younger and buying my first house.

All three services have a better alternative. Switching to these saved me a great deal of money that would otherwise have gone to needless expenses with diminishing returns. Without those savings, I wouldn't have felt comfortable enough to explore the wealth creation strategies we'll cover in later chapters. That is why it is our first step: It opens to door to better things.

Getting a Better Mortgage, Brokers, and More

We aren't replacing the service of a mortgage, but rather where we get it from. When we're looking to get money for our first home, our first instinct is a mortgage offered by our bank. After all, mortgages are one of the longest-running, slowest-burning, but most reasonable-looking loans we can have.

Mortgages take a house we would never have been able to afford on our own, and give us the power to start living in it for a reasonable monthly rate. When I went to my bank for my first mortgage, I signed everything they put in front of me, while understanding pretty much none of it.

A couple of years down the road, my financial situation got difficult, and my bank couldn't help in a meaningful way, so, for the first time, I thought about speaking to an independent advisor.

It turned out that the mortgage I'd taken out, while pretty normal, was adding to my problems. I was put in touch with a mortgage broker, which was like having my eyes opened to a whole new world. While a bank will typically only offer its own mortgage plans, a broker can show us a plethora of available options, and help us get in touch with whoever is offering the best choices.

All I had to do was ask my broker to switch my mortgage from the bank's to a new one I wanted. Although the principal amount of money I had to pay didn't change, the way that payment was divided, and the far lower interest rate, meant that I ended up saving thousands of dollars in the long run. Even when my new monthly mortgage payments conveniently offered to roll up and combine my property taxes,—which had previously been socking it to me to the tune of about $2,000 a year—I still ended up paying less per month than I had been previously. This led to a snowball effect as all the money I saved through that switch could now be invested, and the effect of that is strongly felt in my life today.

Always find a broker who comes very well-recommended. Ask what fees we need to pay them and, for the love of all-holy green-and-viscous *cow cud*, take our time in deciding what rates are best for us. Don't just take the first option we find. The greatest benefit of a broker is that they can find almost every mortgage option available. Let's use that.

Brokers are also great for helping us to invest. Aside from mortgages, they are comfortable browsing through all sorts of investment markets, particularly the stock market. While a lot of brokers are content just to perform the orders we give them, most modern brokers are more than happy to perform double-duty as financial advisors in their own right.

Between brokers and regular advisors, it becomes easy to form well-rounded opinions on what to do with our money, so long as they're fully licensed. For instance, a US broker must be licensed with both FINRA and the SEC. Always do the homework.

Brokers not only help us invest but also diversify. Diversification is a great way to reduce the risks of strategies such as

Stacy's mutual funds, or Roy and Annie's retirement account. For instance, having a smaller stake in two mutual funds in unrelated industries would've given Stacy more stable security than her large stake in a single fund. Double stakes would have also made it easier for her to abandon ship and reinvest in a better one when the time came.

What About Mortgage Life Insurance?

To be clear: A mortgage is a good thing, and life insurance is a good thing. Mortgage life insurance, on the other hand...

"That's a whole 'nuther animal," as Dad used to say.

It is a reassuring feeling to get insured, and equally satisfying to be called a "policyholder" by our bank. That's one of those labels that make us feel that we've officially "made it" as an adult. Thus, when our bank offers to include mortgage life insurance in the monthly payments of our first home, it just feels like an extra layer of security for a nominal fee.

What's the difference between mortgage life insurance and standard life insurance? From a bank's perspective, the primary difference is that it's either illegal for them to sell life insurance, or else heavily regulated and restricted. Mortgage life insurance was developed as a legal workaround that has the added benefit of being an easy upsell for the bank.

Unlike a standard policy, mortgage life insurance doesn't offer a tax-free cash payout to a beneficiary when we die. Instead, it fully pays off the mortgage balance still owing on our home.

While it might seem responsible, and even charitable, to know that whoever we are leaving our house to won't have to pay a dime for it in the event of our death, there are three major problems with this if we do a little homework.

Problem 1: Our beneficiary gets a free house, but that's it.

They could just as easily get a lump sum of tax-free cash—equivalent to the balance owing on the home, along with a considerable amount extra—from any decent life insurance policy, whether whole life or term. Mortgages are some of the easiest and slowest-burning debts to manage, especially with a good broker. Opting for mortgage insurance over a standard policy is like being a nurse who treats the guy with a papercut before she pays any attention to the purple-faced guy who's complaining of a stabbing chest pain that keeps radiating into his left arm.

Life insurance policies allow us to decide where the death benefit will be paid. For example, many policyholders leave directions for their mortgage to be paid off first, then pay any other large debts, and finally, pay the remainder to a beneficiary. Death brings expenses, particularly if the decedent was the household's primary source of income. Funerals alone can cost thousands of dollars... a truly disgusting fact when you stop and think about it.

But millions of people still elect for mortgage life insurance. Is there a silver lining?

Fun fact: Nope!

Problem 2: Mortgage life insurance pays out less money the longer we pay into it.

Normally, the providing bank will arrange for the insurance premium to be conveniently rolled up into our regular mortgage payment, so we're still only making one monthly payment. However, we're paying extra for diminishing returns: The longer we make payments, the smaller the balance left owing on our mortgage. And the less the bank has to pay out if we happen to kick it.

It's pretty obvious why banks love this, but the whole idea of insurance is that we should see growing rewards for long-term contributions, not penalization. Standard policies promise a larger payout in exchange for long-term payment of our premiums. Mortgage life insurance is a complete reversal of that.

Problem 3: Mortgage life insurance pays out the balance owing on mortgages in just 12% of all claims.

TWELVE. FREAKING. PERCENT. 88% of the time, the issuing bank is content to just take our money, promise to pay a consistently lowering amount, and then refuse to even do that.

Numbers are nothing without human faces relating to them. 100 people died. 100 families lost a loved one. 12 families got a paid-off home. 88 families were told, "No."

Now multiply those people exponentially until we have national statistics.

Mortgage life insurance is high-risk and low-benefit. It just isn't worth it. There are far better types of insurance out there, such as ACTUAL life insurance, health insurance, disability insurance, critical illness insurance, and estate planning. These can all be invaluable when we need them, help us tackle urgent overwhelming circumstances, and are open to rewarding us for being a long-term contributor... sometimes even before we die, as in the case of cash-value insurance. We'll discuss insurance options further in Chapter 8.

Meanwhile, in the Land of Credit...

Credit cards are the third bank-given service that should trigger alarm bells whenever they're offered. Like mortgages, credit cards can be helpful and have even become necessary for such modern conveniences as airline and hotel reservations, online shopping, and even security deposits. Also like mortgages, it's vital we don't just accept the first set of terms offered.

There is wisdom in having no more than one card at a time. Banks and credit card companies love to go wild with offers, and, if we are too quick to accept, we'll easily end up with three or more cards, all of them crying out to be used.

It is stressful having to keep track of multiple sources of debt, and that stress can lead to a lot of wasted time and energy as we get bogged down in uncertainty. If we're in this situation, the best thing we can do is consolidate our credit balances.

What this means is taking out a loan on a lower interest rate than most of our cards and other debts, yet also large enough to pay off all of them. Yes, we still owe just as much money after taking the consolidation loan as we did before, but now we only owe it to one institution, and we are paying one low-interest rate. We have a variety of loan options: A consolidation loan, a repayment plan arranged by a debt consolidation company, a line of credit, or a lower-interest credit card.

I cannot recommend consolidation strategies enough, as many credit cards out there charge over 20% interest. This is what I call "high," but what the typical bank in the US might call "average." Paying 2o% or more in interest can get ridiculous when we consider the things we use credit cards for: Food, clothes, entertainment, and other consumables that don't generate long-term value.

Paying with credit instead of cash means making life much more expensive without meaningfully raising its quality. Consolidation is the first step towards breaking a bad credit habit.

Tips on Consolidation

Unfortunately, some lending institutions really enjoy getting our regular high-interest payments and will not authorize a consolidation loan to be negotiated. If we're unable to consolidate our credit but have a steady income, there's another way to get our credit under control, called the Debt Avalanche. In this method, we make the required minimum payments to our credit debt and other loans, but then use any extra money we have to make overpayments on the one debt with the highest interest rate. We keep doing this until that debt is fully paid off, and then we move on to overpaying the debt with the second-highest interest. And then the next. If we can maintain paying the same amount we began the Avalanche with, our subsequent debts will be paid off much faster as each subsequent debt gets more money paid to it per month until it is eliminated.

For a simple example, let's say that we have three credit cards with large balances owing: One with 25% interest, one with 15% interest, and one with 8% interest. All of them have minimum payments of $100 a month, so we pay a total of $300 a month. We can budget out an additional $50 a month for an overpayment,—for a new total of $350 a month—so we now can pay $150 a month toward the 25% interest card. If the 25% card also carries the largest balance, then this method is doubly beneficial. Then we simply continue to pay $350 a month until the Avalanche is complete.

When the 25% card is fully paid off, our best option is to cancel it. If we still have balances owing on the other two cards,—which we may or may not, as the payment priority is based on the cards' interest rates and not the total balance owing—we then immediately move on to paying the same monthly amount of $350, but now focusing an overpayment of $250 onto our 15% card. Once that card is paid off, we cancel it and move on to our final debt—the 8% card—towards which we are now paying the full $350 a month, $250 more than its required minimum payment.

We can see how this is a fantastic method for keeping our interest rates from spiraling out of control, which is the single greatest danger of credit cards: Spiraling interest on a credit card is the evil twin of compounding interest on an investment.

By the time we are done, we will have paid off all of our credit card debt at an expedited rate, canceled any superfluous cards, and be left with only a single low-interest card. If managed carefully, this can save years of payments and thousands of dollars in interest.

Another method to consider is the Debt Snowball, which follows the same process as the Debt Avalanche, except that we focus the initial overpayment on the debt with the smallest balance owing. When that debt is paid, we continue paying the same amount every month, but the increased overpayment is now dedicated to the next-smallest debt. By the time we have only our largest debt remaining, we will likely be overpaying it by hundreds of dollars a month, which can also eliminate all debt in an expedited time frame.

The Debt Snowball and Debt Avalanche can work for a wide variety of debts, but, as a general rule, the Debt Avalanche is preferable when we have a wider range of interest rates, which is why it is recommended for credit card debt. If our interest rates are comparable across all debts, then the Debt Snowball is less of a risk and is also generally easier to keep track of, as our debt primacy is simply arranged in ascending order.

In either case, the key is to decide on a total monthly payment which we can easily manage over a prolonged period of time— the combined minimum payments of all cards or debts, plus a small initial overpayment—and then keep paying that same amount every month until all debt is gone.

What Should We Do Next?

Once our debt is consolidated, simplify immediately. Keep one credit card with a low-interest rate and preferably a low spending limit. If we want to make a large purchase, we can simply continue the Avalanche or Snowball even after all our debt has been eliminated: To carry on with the previous example, we would then have a fully paid-off credit card and we would be putting an additional $350 of free cash into it every month that can be spent without penalty of interest or debt, while still racking up any reward points our card offers. If we are saving up for specific short-term purchases, rather than long-term investments, this is a very easy way to do it.

Remember, we can often overpay credit cards or lines of credit indefinitely, so a low spending limit is not necessarily prohibitive to our purchases, and far less likely to turn into a monster: It is far safer to have a credit card with a $1,500 spending limit and $5,000 overpaid onto it than it is to just have a card with a $6,500 spending limit. Both cards can buy that $6,500 fishing boat, but one will leave us with only $1,500 in debt while the other will leave us with $6,500 in debt.

Having more cards on hand just adds the temptation of outright maxing them before we rein ourselves in. Lower spending capacity and lower interest mean that we'll be less likely to push ourselves beyond our means, and less likely to curse our decisions later on. Having only one card means we'll also be more likely to stop sooner before our debt situation feels too insurmountable and we need another consolidation.

For me, the most effective method is to keep my remaining credit card frozen. And that's literal, not a cute way of saying call the bank to put a hold on spending: Literally put your credit card in an airtight container, put that in a bucket of water, and put it in your freezer. If we need it, we have to thaw it.

90% of the time, by the time the card is thawed out, we realize that we didn't need the item anyway. That may sound crazy, but it's not. Almost *everything* we buy with credit cards is an impulse item.

Bottom Line

While our bank certainly can have the best products for our needs, it doesn't help to rush in. That's how we end up with steep mortgage rates, unhelpful insurance schemes, and too many dang credit cards.

The important thing to say is, "Thanks. I'll think about it."

This gives us time to do our research, talk to an advisor, and use modern technology like the Internet to get a wider perspective on what the world has to offer. Rushing in while ignoring the alarm bells is how they get you.

4

SMASH THE HIERARCHY:
REVERSING OUR THINKING ON THE FIRST PLACES WE SHOULD BE CONTRIBUTING OUR MONEY TO.

There's the traditional way of investment focus and debt repayment, but we'll soon see that there's quite a difference between the traditional way and what actually works.

Step 2: Embrace the Concept of Using Other People's Money.

I hope you have both a strong stomach and a strong love of beef steak because I'm going to tell you in grim detail a war story from my youth: The Battle of Ear-Tag D17.

D17 was a mild-mannered Black Angus/Hereford-crossed "Black Baldy" cow—black body, white face, with a much-in-demand marbling quality—who inexplicably became a homicidal lunatic 18 seconds after giving birth to her first bull calf. A lot of cows get overprotective of their babies, but this psychopath was one for the annuls of cowboy history. Black Baldies are a notably passive breed, perhaps because they do not fully comprehend how delicious they are. Cutting against either the grain or knowledge base of the breed, D17 must have known exactly how delectable her newborn veal was destined to be because she put me through a wooden-planked wind fence the first time I approached her floundering neonate to check his airway for amniotic fluid. Not only was it EXCRUCIATINGLY PAINFUL, but it was also maternally negligent: Baby cows drown in their own amniotic fluid all the time!

During her magical first two weeks of motherhood, D17 managed to trample almost every member of my family. At one point, I considered giving her an actual name as opposed to just her ear-tag designation,—and had even narrowed my choices down to either a notably berserk Viking warrior from my distant ancestry or the *Enola Gay*—but it was my older brother who eventually said, "We don't speak the name of the devil."

Blue-haired animal lovers with no comprehension of just how epic a tomahawk steak can be may shriek like harpies when I tell them this next part, but I quickly ditched my traditional cattle cane in favor of a 2x4 every time I was required to venture into the maternity pasture. Cattle canes are constructed from a sturdy plastic polymer that can be used to guide or prod inattentive calves on cattle drives and can also give a stinging *Whack!* to their defiant mamas when necessary. However, when dealing with bovine juggernauts, a 2x4 has a little more stopping power.

The Battle of Ear-Tag D17 took place on what would normally be a 10-minute cattle drive, moving about 30 pairs of new calves and their mothers from the maternity pen to the south pasture. The adorable naivety of cattle canes had become a thing of the distant past, and every member of my family was now packing 2x4s. D17 saw us coming through the gate and met us at full stride.

For the next 30 minutes, the battle raged in a whirling dervish of literal blood, sweat, and tears, topped with an occasional spray of manure. (Not sure if you're aware, but cows will "fury poop" when sufficiently agitated) Heroes arose, cowards fled, ballads were inspired, and we had barely progressed 20 feet closer to the south gate.

My 2x4 had gone MIA in the chaos—or perhaps D17 had eaten it in an attempt to absorb her enemy's life force— and my nemesis could immediately smell my weakness. Abandoning her trampling of Dad for a moment,—which I'm sure he appreciated —she locked onto me like a laser-guided missile and charged.

The skull of a charging cow is basically an 800 lb anvil coming at you at 20mph, and I was too far away from the fence to clamber to safety. All I had time to do was snatch up a nearby boulder—which I probably could not have budged from the ground in a less adrenaline-fuelled circumstance—and lob it straight up in the air like a mortar round.

To the great surprise of both of us, the boulder dropped straight down onto the crown of D17's head with resonating *"BONK!"* Her charge was stopped on a dime, which seemed to fly in defiance of most laws of physics. For a long moment, two bug-eyed foes stared at one another in stunned silence as the rock dropped to the ground like the hammer of Thor. Then D17's front legs buckled underneath her, and she pitched forward with her jaw in the dirt and butt in the air like a terrified peasant prostrating before the emperor.

"BAAAAAAAAAWWWLL!!!" she announced, which I later learned was the bovine term for unconditional surrender, but which I initially mistook for a death knell.

"Holy crap, I killed her!" I blurted.

Then D17 rose to her feet, shook her head a couple of times, led her oblivious offspring to the south gate leading to greener pastures... and never bothered anyone again for the remainder of her many years on the ranch.

I don't know if you'd call it cognitive recalibration, mild brain damage, or just a Windows update. Whatever the designation, it was a brutally transformative moment that changed everyone's life for the better, including hers, and led to a happier future.

I bring this up because, looking back on my love-hate relationship with so many aspects of finance, I think it's sometimes necessary to have something similar happen to us to reevaluate our financial planning. Getting a similar butt-kicking on a psychological level can do our wallets a world of good.

The Rock

The three stories we covered earlier are all good examples of cow-bonking rocks, and they all send a clear message: How we're doing things now—and even historically—isn't necessarily how we should be doing things going forward.

At the time of this writing, most people are throwing the first fruits of their paycheck into paying down mortgages and other debts. Fair enough. We all want to be debt-free.

Conventional wisdom states that a mortgage is the most important debt to pay off first because it's the biggest and therefore most scary. The second priority is any secondary debts. Then we'll pay into a child's college fund, life insurance, and, a long way down the road, maybe we'll consider contributions to an IRA or RRSP. In the interests of parallel strategies within this book, we will often refer to those two investment tools collectively as IRA/RRSPs due to their strong similarities.

After-tax funds such as Roth IRAs and TFSAs—which we will likewise refer to collectively as Roth/TFSAs in circumstances where they have closely aligned uses in both the US and Canada —are viewed as the lowest priority of all, and many times they are never even considered. When hard times arise, they are often the first monthly expense to be canceled.

The bonk on the head we got from the three stories in Chapter 2 should tell us that a complete reversal of these priorities has become necessary. We live in the Land of Opportunity, and we need to make the most of that.

A strategy that has been gaining a lot of momentum in recent years puts the investment primacy on Roth/TFSAs, followed by insurance products. Both of these, when handled well, are great ways to grow our investments for later in life. Using this model, only after our Roth/TFSAs are maxed out should our conventional IRA/RRSPs be tended to.

Our mortgage, because it has a low interest rate and relatively well-spaced installments, simply does not need to be a priority, no matter how big and scary it may appear.

Of course, we must still make the payments needed to eventually clear what we owe on our house, but strategies such as mortgage prepayment and overpayments can be avoided altogether while still enabling us to save and invest respectably. We do not necessarily benefit from clearing our mortgage early, and we might even lose out on huge investment growth. As in all cases, our circumstances will differ, and some people have been very happy paying off their mortgage early. However, bear with me for a moment, and let's see if another option makes sense to you.

First, we need to get comfortable with spending other people's money.

Other People's Money

Other People's Money, or OPM. My first experience with this phrase occurred when I was a kid. A local businessman from Texas liked to claim that OPM was his secret to success, and he may have been telling the truth. I'll probably never know for certain, because he was shortly thereafter accused of defrauding his business partners and employees, and fled the country. I'm not sure if he eventually ended up in a mansion or a gutter, but, either way, the OPM acronym left a bad taste in my mouth.

Even outside of that experience, the term sounds slightly sinister and self-serving when taken out of context. But the fact is that virtually everyone utilizes OPM, and we use it almost every day of our lives. Any form of loan, mortgage, or credit technically fits that designation.

People like to offer their money all the time... but only so long as it's on credit. Credit and home mortgages are the most common forms of OPM. Usually, credit agreements are set up to chiefly benefit the lender, but, if we know what we're doing, we can use the money they give us to not only procure important amenities, such as a house to stay in but also divert money into places that will generate far more value for us in the long run. Now, investing in leverage like this can be quite risky, so we don't want to rush anything or get emotional while doing it. (Be under no illusion: HGTV programs lie to all of us about the "indescribable joy" of homeownership.) Let's break things down together.

Firstly, when I talk about leverage, I'm not talking about borrowing money to invest straight into something else. What I'm saying is that when we take out a mortgage or if we happen to already have some other large slow-burning debt, paying it all off right away isn't our only option.

A lot of people think paying every spare dollar they have into removing debts right away is the best idea or even the only responsible action for their family. At the time, it often seems like a great idea. This is because people often believe that the only alternative is reckless spending, along with mounting interest and a never-ending rack-up of debt.

So, fearing this one extreme, we are tempted to swing to the other, to the point where we wind up paying off our home an entire decade ahead of schedule, and our credit card debt even earlier than that.

This is a tempting prospect for sure. A whole decade of no interest building up against us? An early return to being debt-free? That sounds fantastic.

However, there are notable alternatives to this strategy, or rather to this blind refusal to maximize the potential of our OPM. Even if we are this aggressive at paying off our house, we're still going to take about 15 years at best to do so. And during that time, because every spare dollar is going into clearing our house debt in under two decades, we're also having around 15 years of absolutely zero growth in our savings.

We'll be 15 years closer to retirement age without anything meaningful in the bank to show for it. We'll have the relief of not being in the red, or being in debt, but not necessarily for long. I think we can do better than that.

Try this: When we're in mortgage debt, instead of aggressively paying it all back as quickly as possible, simply make the minimum payments required. That's the first thing we do.

Next, take the non-linear approach. People like to work in a sequential, "one after the other" sort of way with their money. This is why Debt Snowball and Debt Avalanche strategies are so popular, and, to be clear, I am not diminishing the value of those strategies, particularly for people struggling with excessive debt. They work by tackling one thing at a time in a logical order. In fact, the method I'm going to describe next is a variation inspired directly by those strategies: Maximizing the potential of OPM while making only minimum payments.

When we're comfortable with OPM, we can put our extra money into growth accounts while simultaneously keeping our debt under control.

So, we'll be working with our money in a staggered way, putting some of it on one side to meet our requirements with debt, while putting the rest on the other side to start growing and generating long-term returns. There's no reason why we can't do these two things at the same time. Being debt-free is not a prerequisite for making meaningful investments and generating meaningful growth. If it was, we'd see far fewer entrepreneurs setting themselves up for quick success, as many of them have to take on debt to get the equipment necessary for their business. Even the most successful titans of industry often carry a lot of debt, which puzzled me when I was younger: Why would billionaires still have debt? Was their wealth actually a sham or scam?

No. They just know how to make a ton of money while paying their debts in the most efficient way possible.

So, like the billionaires, we need to retrain our brains to be comfortable with staggering money in this way. No one says we have to take big risks. Most of us aren't setting up an international real estate empire: We're just doing a little simple math. In this chapter, I'll be giving mathematical examples of great OPM management in action, so we can see how it works.

Some Rules About OPM

OPM is a great way to smash the "hierarchy of primacy" which we have all been lulled into thinking is just the way things are. Let's say we have a 25-year mortgage on our home, and we know that, with a little budgeting, belt-tightening, and overpayment, we could reduce that amortization period by 10 years.

Make the minimum payments instead.

And let's be clear about that. That means making only 1 full mortgage payment every month. Don't even switch to the biweekly payment system which gives us 13 full payments per year, and shaves off one year in every twelve from our amortization period. Yes, it would mean paying off our house in the full 25 years instead of the 15 that can be so tempting. However, the investment interest we can generate in our favor over those same 25 years through contributing to growth accounts will more than makeup for having to pay interest on our house for an extra decade.

Using OPM means we cannot clear all our debts as quickly, so it's important to know when to use it.

Rules:

1. We only use OPM, staggering our money between debt and growth contributions, when our debts are low-interest. A mortgage is a great example of low-interest debt. Some credit cards, and even car payments or payment plans on home furnishings, may also have a low enough APR to work as a source of OPM.

2. Always think twice before using OPM if it means delaying high-interest debt, such as that from a high-interest credit card. If the growth account we're contributing to has a lower rate of return than the debt we have to pay off, we're going to have a hard time, or even risk seeing our high-interest debt spiral rapidly beyond what we've budgeted for. The better solution is

to Avalanche or Snowball our debt until we only have low-interest debts remaining, and switch back to staggering OPM from there.

3. In some cases, both strategies can overlap and save precious time if we have sufficient funds and can budget them both carefully: We can initiate an OPM strategy for our investments and low-interest debt while simultaneously enacting an Avalanche or Snowball strategy for our higher-interest debts. If we can do this successfully, we may be in an even better position once our highest-interest debts are eliminated, i.e., we will be accustomed to budgeting overpayments, so we can then divert those previous payments toward our OPM strategy. However, if we do not have sufficient income to overlap strategies without stretching our money too thin, just do them sequentially: Eliminate high-interest debt first, then use OPM for what's left.

Now, here are some reasons why using OPM can be so good when dealing with mortgage debt in particular:

Firstly, we don't get anything tangible out of paying off our home. It becomes easier to sell once it's fully paid off, but even so, it's not easy to quickly convert where we live into cash when we fall on hard times and need to support ourselves with drastic actions. In other words, our home is likely our most valuable asset but also has the lowest liquidity.

So, aggressively paying off our mortgage, even when all other debts are out the way, can leave us quite brittle to outside tragedies. Our home will also almost certainly lose value over time due to the way real estate works, meaning our home just isn't a great appreciating investment, even if we regularly maintain and renovate it. It's great at keeping us warm and safe, but we already get both those perks even while we're paying it all off. Even the increased value from maintenance and renovations are only really worth the time and expense if we can be reasonably confident that they are adding at least 1.5x our investment, or even double, to our home value: For every $1,000 we spend on fixing up the place, we should be able to add at least $1,500 to our asking price., and $2,000 is better. As a home ages, this is not always possible. No matter how many improvements we've made to an ancestral property, some buyers will always show a preference for a new home.

We need to value a home for what it is: A place we can proudly call our own, and even pass on to our kids. In a financial downturn, it might become a burden if we haven't planned sufficiently in other areas. Using OPM to invest can leave us with a handy source of cash for when the going gets tough, and prepare us to enjoy our castle throughout a prosperous retirement.

Next, because paying off a mortgage even at max speed takes so long, it's important to also consider inflation. A dollar today is worth less than a dollar yesterday. The dollar of tomorrow will be worth even less. This isn't just me being a doomer, or boomer, or whatever it is the kids are saying these days. This is just how it is for economies worldwide. Inflation happens, and, when it does, individual banknotes buy less: Less electricity, less water, less bread, you name it. The pace of inflation will often even outpace the interest rate of our bank's High-Interest Savings Account, as we will discuss further in Chapter 5.

Because the minimum rates of a mortgage don't change, and can even be reduced with help from a broker, this means we're effectively paying less each month. If we have to pay a minimum of $900 per month for 25 years, then that's what we'll still pay to the end, even when inflation means that $900 is only effectively worth $600 by the end. In this way, inflation can work in a long-term mortgage's favor, especially when we consider that most long-term employees will also see pay increases over the years: Their wages go up as the value of their mortgage payment comes down.

Likewise, the interest we think we're saving by paying off the mortgage early is likely going to matter a lot less than we think, again because of inflation. Even if inflation only occurs at a rate of 2% each year,—again more than most High-Interest Savings Accounts can offer as compensation—over 15 years on an aggressive mortgage payoff, that's still enough to make, say, a $70,000 saving on interest worth tens of thousands of dollars less.

On the flip side, growth accounts and investment accounts are great ways of effectively preserving and even increasing the value of our money despite inflation. The sooner we put money in such a place, the sooner we're protecting its value from the ravages of time which, as we'll see below, will be far more impactful in the long run.

Math Time: Being Aggressive

Before I show the math behind using OPM properly, let's look at the scenario of an ambitious power couple who thought three caramel macchiatos at Starbucks were a better investment than this book.

We're going to use a very simple example where things like inflation or interest variation don't exist. Because we aren't factoring for inflation, our results from this example will be better in practice than they look here. However, it's important to note that while our example will use a fixed mortgage for simplicity, not all mortgages have unchanging interest rates, i.e., many fixed-rate mortgages will be subject to change after 5 years. For that reason, we always take our time, read the fine print, and ask lots of questions for understanding before we sign off on such a big loan, and never forget the option of using the services of a mortgage broker to find the best rates, even years from now.

Now, imagine that we're first-time homebuyers looking at acquiring a $250,000 mortgage loan. According to the offered contract, we'll be charged a consistent 4% interest, with minimum monthly payments totaling $1,188.80. This means we'll be paying off $14,265.60 a year, and our debt will be fully paid off in, um… 30 years. Any first-time homeowner will surely cringe when they think about paying $1,188.80 each month for 30 years, and this is what leads to the natural, but sub-optimal, urge to aggressively pay off our mortgages at an expedited rate.

Let's assume that we, the power couple, are young and married. We're respected professionals, and we don't want to be paying off our new house for 30 years. So we commit to paying the whole dang thing off in 20.

To pay off our house 10 years earlier, we'd need to put another $321.82 towards it each month. Added onto the minimum monthly rate, that's $1,510.62 we'll be paying each month, just for our home loan. For the moment, we assume that going higher than that wouldn't be comfortable for us, which is reasonable.

That extra $321.82 will amount to an extra $3,861.84 spent each year. Maybe this seems a little steep, but we know we can meet that faster pace, and fully owning our house a decade earlier is tempting, so we do it.

Partway through, we decide to go hard or go home. Why pay only once a month, when we can instead pay once a fortnight? We re-space our payment schedule, decide to skip Starbucks for a while, and we are now eking out $19,638.06 towards our mortgage each year, an impressive annual increase of $5,372.46. This is the point where we've gone full-on aggressive, and have little or nothing to spare for savings at the moment. But we're good at sticking to plans once we've made them, so we can do it. And it means we can now pay off our home in 18 years instead of 20.

We do it. It's 18 years later, we fully own our home, and we're feeling pretty happy. Also, our family has expanded, and we now have a 12-year old daughter, Li'l Sue. We decide that our disciplined overpayments have prepared us to now build our savings. Being familiar with the concept of both the Debt Snow-ball and Debt Avalanche, we agree that the same amount we used to spend on mortgage payments can now just get dropped into a growth account instead. We've got our groove on, we've kept up with all other living expenses, and it feels like a breeze to begin investing at a rate of $1,636.50 a month. That's an impressive amount for any family to put away for retirement.

Imagine we are Canadian,—stay with me, America, this applies equally as we'll see—and therefore have our choice of HISAs, TFSAs, and RRSPs. HISAs don't have the interest rate that we'd hope for, so that one's out, which leaves us with a choice between TFSAs and RRSPs, and the "TF" portion of TFSA is immediately intriguing. However, much like the Roth IRA, a TFSA only allows us to invest $6,000 in it per year without any serious penalties... namely full-rate taxation on the entire contribution amount. So, to our dismay, we find our ability to save being bottlenecked.

Now, we could split our investments, putting $6,000 into a TFSA and the remaining $13,638.06 into an RRSP, although that feels a little more complicated than necessary. However, we then realize that an RRSP allows up to 18% of our pre-tax income to be contributed to it. Let's say we've been earning a combined gross income of $120,000 a year. In that case, our contribution limit is $21,600. Awesome! Our entire investment budget is less than that, $19,638.06. So we can quite comfortably sink everything we used to put into mortgage payments into an RRSP instead, without fear of penalty as we're still under the contribution threshold. Forget that silly TFSA and its measly $6,000 contribution cap...

We find a good RRSP fund with a consistent 8% rate of return, and faithfully make contributions to it for the next 12 years. So, 30 years after we first took that mortgage loan, we end up with full homeownership and a cool $372,672.81 tucked away. Well, almost... It's closer to $223,603.69 after the 40% in back-end taxes are paid. Kind of makes us wish we could have utilized that TFSA instead.

This same situation for a couple in the good old US of A would be even more tricky as both IRAs and Roth IRAs have a contribution cap of $6,000 a year, which increases to $7,000 a year for those over the age of 50, which in our example was 3 years ago. We can own multiple IRAs, but their combined contribution totals cannot exceed $6,000 or $7,000 a year. By this time, we realize that our best option is to skip the income tax breaks of the traditional IRA in favor of the tax-free withdrawals of the Roth IRA, so our annual investments of $19,638.06 would be divided as follows: $6,000 in a Roth IRA with impressive 8% returns, and, thinking that the rest is just gravy, we decide to simply dump the balance of $13,638.06 into a High-Interest Savings Account earning an impressive—for a bank—2% a year.

After 9 years, we begin putting $7,000 a year into our Roth IRA, and only $12,638.06 into our HISA. At the end of our 12 years of investments,—and after the interest earned in our HISA is hit every year at the marginal tax rate on our tax return—we will have a paid-off home and tax-deducted cash amounting to about $297,097.57. And we just turned 53, and Li'l Sue just started her second year of college.

Now, when we factor in other things such as promotions, pay raises, and pension funds, this doesn't look like a bad outcome, and, to be fair, it is far more of an accomplishment than many families will ever achieve.

But I can do you one better.

Math Time: Using OPM

I'm about to hit you in the head with a rock.

Let's rewind our clock by 30 years. We're now 23 years old again, we actually skipped the three trips to Starbucks and bought this book instead, and we're looking over our mortgage for this same house. Paying it all off in 18 years would mean spending $19,638.06 per year on the mortgage. But paying it across the full 30-year amortization period means spending only $14,265.60 a year.

However, we are still willing to work hard for our future. We could still afford to pay the $19,638.06 into the mortgage, but instead of doing that, we're just going to make the minimum payments, leaving us with an additional $5,372.46 each year to invest where we wish. That's low enough to fit snugly into a Roth IRA or TFSA without any penalties since both allow us to make annual contributions of $6,000. Our advisor finds us a Roth/TFSA with a fantastic average return rate of 8%, just like in our last scenario, so we place our additional $5,372.46 into it each year... for the next 30 years. While we can only put so much into one of these accounts each year, there's no limit to how much the accounts can hold in total.

This money will remain tax-exempt, even when we withdraw it, so we can be confident that it won't be ripped from us as we make withdrawals in retirement.

That's $5,372.46 a year, broken down into small payments of $447.70(2) per month. In 30 years, it will grow into a tax-free pool of $608,605.44.

We're now 53 again. But, in America, we have more than double the amount of money we would have had after-tax if we went with the aggressive repayment method and over 3.75x more than if we had just tucked away that extra $5,372.46 into a sock drawer every year. In Canada, although we come out with the same $608,605.44 in both countries, we'd have earned almost 3x more than we would have with the aggressive 18-year plan.

One last "BONK!" for the road...

And this is the big one.

Rental properties are often viewed as the absolute worst form of OPM, as we don't have a home to call our own, no matter how long we keep shoveling in payments. A fair argument is that only the landlord collecting rent is benefiting from OPM.

However, quite a few years back, it occurred to me that paying rent can cost considerably less than mortgage payments, and also has far fewer associated expenses. Knowing something about how small amounts can yield huge returns in the right circumstances, I decided to dig a little deeper.

Here's a fun little hypothetical.

How much money could we save in 30 years if we chose to just rent a modest home or apartment, paying a single flat rate that often includes our utilities? What if we based our savings plan on the same model that we know we can afford from the aggressive strategy on a $250,000 mortgage in our example, i.e, $19,638.06 a year? Except now, instead of making monthly payments of $1,188.80 and putting the additional $447.70 into our investment savings, we're only paying $950 in rent and putting away $686.50(5) a month, or $8,238.06 a year. Over 30 years, we contribute a total of $247,141.80 to our investment funds.

Our combined fund balance is $940,141.95.

And that's not counting the additional utility payments, home insurance, renovations, and property taxes associated with the homeowner's mortgage. Let's conservatively say that those average out to around $4,000 a year. Factor those into our plan, and now we're paying $950 in rent and putting away $1,019.84 a month. $12,238.06 a year.

In both of these rental scenarios, we exceed our $6,000 Roth/TFSA contribution cap for the year, so we may have to put some of our investments into back-end tax funds. In the second example, where we factor in the additional $4,000 in homeowner payments, we would end up owing the most tax in Canada, but even that worst-case scenario is far more manageable. Let's assume that we manage to invest the full amount of $12,238.06 across a variety of funds every year, again at an average rate of return of 8%: We put $6,000 a year into a Roth/TFSA and $6,238.06 a year into a Roth 401(k) or RRSP, both of which have high contribution caps, although the RRSP will have back-end taxes owing. For the sake of a worst-case scenario, we will set the back-end taxes at 40%. ($19,500 can be paid annually into a Roth 401(k) and $27,830 into an RRSP.)

In 30 years, we'd have invested a total of $367,141.80, and we'd have $1,396,631.30: Well over one million dollars more than we invested. Minus $284,760.28 in back-end tax if we're in Canada.

Even the Canadians still end up with a net total of $1,111,871.02.

Don't believe everyone who says that renting does nothing but shovel your money into a bottomless pit.

The Takeaways

The most important thing to note from the preceding examples —the family who chose aggressive mortgage payments, the family who opted for the full amortization of their mortgage, and the family who chose a modest rental property—is that all three families utilized the same amount of money, budgeted from the same household income, over the same 30-year time-span: In both of the mortgage scenarios, the families paid $19,636.06, divided between their mortgage and investments, plus $4,000 in associated homeowner costs. In the rental scenario, the same total of $23,636.06 was divided only between rental payments and investments.

The aggressive "I'll pay it off in 18 years" family invested $19,638.06 into growth accounts for 12 years after their primary debt was cleared, putting in a total of $235,656.72. After-tax, their fund values totaled less than $300,000. In fact, the Canadian couple who only utilized their RRSP *lost* $12,053.03 after-tax, because they did not have sufficient growth time to offset their tax rate. ($235,656.72 - $223,603.69 = $12,053.03) By 53 years old, they didn't have any meaningful growth to show for their investment despite investing so much. This is because they started late.

Our alternative couple who said, "They gave us 30 years, so we'll use 30 years" wound up much better. They always had a little leftover to contribute to growth from the very beginning.

At an investment rate of only $447.70 per month, they only invested $161,172 in total over 30 years. They got over $600,000 to show for it by the time they turned 53, despite their accounts having the same interest rate as the first family. They simply started earlier. This meant that they more than doubled the returns of the aggressive family while investing just a little more than half as much.

The real moment of cognitive recalibration comes when we learn to handle debt: Use Other People's Money. Now, does getting this long-term reward of doubled savings make an extra 12 years of mortgage payments look worthwhile, or do I need to pick up a bigger rock?

However, both families who took out mortgages also incurred the associated costs of homeownership. They paid an additional $120,000 over 30 years.

And the family who chose to rent a property for the same time could hypothetically see more than twice the investment growth of the homeowners.

Even if the renters eventually decided to buy a $250,000 home, using only their three decades worth of investment returns, they would still have more free cash left over than either of the families who took out a mortgage 30 years earlier: Anywhere between $861,871.02 and $1,146,631.30... whereas the best-case scenario of a mortgage holder was $608,605.44. That's a difference of at least $253,266.58, and at most $538,025.86. I don't know about you, but I wouldn't mind staying in a rental property for a while. Not if I end the day with a fully-paid off home and half a million dollars *more* than everyone else who just finished paying off their long-term mortgage.

To quote that infamous rock from so many decades ago... *"BONK!"*

Slamming huge amounts of money to clear off all our debts early can feel good, but the thinking that inspires it is short-term, not long-term. It is impatient, seeking relatively immediate gratification and relief. In the long-term, this behavior leaves us woefully unprepared and can force us to contribute to taxable accounts which can shave off hundreds of thousands of dollars from our savings and retirement plans.

Long-term success comes neither from paying off all our debts immediately nor from ignoring them entirely. It comes from finding the right balance. This begins with realizing the best way to grow our money early on, and the best help we can seek to assist us in that. It also begins with realizing that not all debts are created equal: APR determines primacy.

While I never suggest letting a high-interest card go unpaid or run untethered, I cannot stress enough that there's no sense in rushing to pay off a good mortgage, either. Let yourself be comfortable with smaller-interest debts, no matter how big and scary their total may seem. It will take a few calculations jotted onto a few napkins, but the rewards can be staggering.

Even if you end up renting your home from a smug landlady who honestly believes that she is the only one benefiting from OPM.

5

ALBERT EINSTEIN VS THE HIGH-INTEREST SAVINGS ACCOUNT:

THE RULE OF 72, AND WHY YOUR BEST BANK ACCOUNT WILL NEVER GET YOU THERE IN TIME.

F rankly, a standard bank account opened early is little better than contributing to a growth account opened late. There's also a reason I mentioned Roth/TFSAs as part of our OPM strategy and not just our regular old savings account. Inflation, low returns, and high tax are simply prohibitive to long-term financial success.

This is probably why some people choose to be aggressive when paying off things like mortgages. They don't always know about good growth accounts until they've already committed several years into their 18-year plan.

Step 3: Learn the Rule of 72.

Brief Backstory Time

As a young man straight out of high school, I had little interest in investment. In my mind, finding a good job with a decent pension, plus a little frugality and savings was enough. However, I didn't quite want to rush off a mortgage in 18 years, either. I wanted to contribute to something, a rainy-day nest egg that could increase in size with manageable contributions over the years.

My first step was to look up a few different High-Interest Savings Accounts in local banks. Some of these accounts offered as much as 2% in annual interest rates, so it seemed like a safe way to grow my money with monthly contributions. As I'd always been taught, a bank's savings account is always a safe place to store and grow my money. The best rate was found in a bank that was not my regular one, so I opened an account there as well: I now had my day-to-day bank, and what I called my "no-touchy" bank. If I had an extra $50 or $100, I threw it into my HISA. By taking even that brief foray beyond my regular bank, I felt a sense of "I'm an adult now!" because I hadn't allowed sentimentality or a meaningless sense of loyalty to hold me back.

Little did I know at the time that the growth rate of an HISA was barely even enough to keep up with inflation, let alone generate additional value for me in the long term. Inflation will regularly outpace the interest of an HISA.

This thought didn't even cross my mind. You see, it wasn't just friends and neighbors saying the bank is a safe place to store my money. The banks were naturally saying the same thing, too. To their credit, they make a compelling argument for the safety and long-term value of their HISAs. An argument that, again, falls flat on its face when we remember that their growth barely keeps up with inflation.

Banks can preserve the value of our money to some extent, but, again, they're not necessarily the best at growing it for us. Their advertising can be brutal though. I remember that, even when I learned I was being charged $5 each time I made a withdrawal, I just shrugged it off and accepted it. I thought the withdrawal fee would teach me discipline, and I felt pretty smug that I was making the so-called responsible choice.

At the time of this writing, my single remaining HISA has exactly $0.50 in it, has maintained that balance for many years, and I frequently forget that it exists. I've moved my money on to greener pastures and left my HISA with the bare minimum needed to stay alive, just in case. And, by "just in case," I mean "just in case I manage to max out the annual contribution cap of literally every other savings option available to me, and still have something left over."

How Does This Relate to the Rule of 72?

A couple of years before the innovation of microwaveable pizza, there lived a man who was a little bit smarter than me. His name was Albert Einstein. Famous for his groundbreaking work in physics,—which remains the intimidating standard for scientists around the world today—his formidable mathematical skills also made him something of a whiz at finance.

He valued and popularized the Rule of 72, which is an easy math tool used to find out how quickly our initial investment or contribution will double in size. All we need to know is our annual interest rate. Our contribution also needs to be benefiting from compounding interest for this tool to work, but compounding interest is by far the most common form in any case. It's what mortgages, car loans, and personal loans use, for instance.

If we aren't sure, just ask what our return rate is based on: Is it just based on the money we initially put in? Or is it based on that initial money plus the interest it earned in previous years? If it's the latter, then we've got compound interest. Most forms of investment give a return rate in compounded interest.

Now, my story relates to the Rule of 72 because, if I'd known this rule, and if I'd used it, I'd have been able to quickly tell that my HISAs were no good for what I wanted them to do: Secure my future.

It's such a great finance tool for the average worker, and it can transform so many financial futures if more people only knew about it.

There is a rumor that Einstein called the Rule of 72 even greater than his discovery of $E=MC^2$. I haven't verified that, but, whether he said it or not, it's certainly had a huge impact on making economics more accessible to the working class.

To use the Rule of 72, we first consider our average annual rate of return. For example, when putting our Roth/TFSA into a growth account, it should have an interest rate of at least 6-8%. These returns are rarely guaranteed, but it is easy for our advisor to backtrack a fund's progress over several years and read its annual report, to find the annual average. Some years will be higher, some lower, and every year will have hills and valleys, but finding an average of 8% or more over 5-10 years means that it is a fund well-worth considering.

We then divide the magical number of 72 by the interest rate. The answer we get is equal to the number of years it will take for our initial contribution to double.

This means we can work out how quickly our money will multiply without even knowing what amount we're putting in yet, so long as we know the interest rate. Because interest is percentage-based, how much money we get scales based on how much we put in. It could be $5 or $500, but it would still take the same amount of time to double based on the same rate.

Now, for a practical example, let's assume we have a basic HISA with an interest rate of 1.5%. That's fairly normal. I was pretty smug with my 2% back in the day, but 1.5% is still decent by HISA standards.

What's 72 divided by 1.5? 48.

If we deposit $100 in that HISA, we'll have a whopping total of $200 waiting for us in the account 48 years later, provided that we never make a withdrawal, since we'll lose $5 in transaction fees each time, and also remembering that inflation will transform that $200 into a fraction of its current value in half a century, perhaps even lower than its initial $100 value. 48 years ago, penny candies were still a thing. You can't get a dang handful of jelly beans out of the dispenser for less than $0.25 now.

Taking things year by year, our deposit of $100 will become $101.50 in 1 year, then $103.02 in the year after that. If our two-year financial review showed a total return on investment of $3.02, we would be firing our advisor and considering legal action.

Now, what if we take another much larger sum, such as the $161,172 invested by our 30-year-mortgage couple in the last chapter? Well, it'll become a respectable $322,344... in 48 years. And we'll be charged for withdrawing it. And it'll be worth less than that because the interest earned is taxed annually at our marginal rate, which means we pay higher income taxes with each passing year. And it will also be even less than that, because, in reality, we're far more likely to deposit the total in small, manageable increments—in this case, $442.70 a month—over 48 years, as opposed to having that full lump sum available all at once, so our annual totals and returns will both be much lower. And, finally, we'll be kicking ourselves anyway, because, thanks to the last chapter, we know that instead of having $322,344 in 48 years, we could've had $608,605.44 in only 30 years by adapting a better strategy from the exact same amount of money.

We know that compound interest can be a truly sexy thing, but it should now be clear beyond rebuttal that HISAs simply aren't fast enough. Just how many 48-year doubling periods do we have in life? A lucky person gets two, and, even then, only if their parents opened the fund for them on the day they were born. Even if we're super-duper lucky like I was and get us some of that sweet, sweet 2% action... our doubling period is still 36 years, and we're only going to get three of those if we live to age 108.

There's never a good reason to store our money in an HISA for very long when our goal is long-term growth. Higher returns are mandatory for a prosperous retirement and a relatively stress-free life leading up to that point. Our HISAs are nothing more than a holding pond while we look for something better.

Make Compound Interest Great Again

Thanks to the Rule of 72, we'll now be able to see at a glance if a contribution we make will be worthwhile, or if it'll grow fast enough to be compatible with our retirement plan. The higher our annual interest, the shorter our doubling period, so let's seek that high-interest sweetness.

A famous comedian once described his long-time faithfulness to his wife by saying, "When you're married to a filet, you don't run around with green baloney." Of course, he ended up having multiple affairs which led to him getting divorced and remarried 3 or 4 times, so he didn't necessarily take his own punchline to heart. But, whatever. It's a great quote that applies equally to both marriage and finding the best investment fund: Your HISA is green baloney.

The next two chapters will be devoted to explaining investment accounts in-depth. Roth/TFSAs are some of the sexiest places to put our money right now, and they're quite easy to understand. But that doesn't mean they don't have a lot of depth to them that needs covering.

Before we go deep, however, let's take another look at just how sexy compound interest in a good investment account can be. Let's take that same $100 we were going to store with the green baloney, and instead, place it into a Roth IRA with an impressive annual return rate of 10%.

After 1 year, our one-time deposit of $100 suddenly becomes $110.

After a total of only 7.2 years, our initial investment will have grown to $200. So, our money can either double in half a century using an HISA, or it can double in less than a decade using a well-invested Roth/TFSA. If we were to let that one-time contribution of $100 sit in our Roth/TFSA for the same 48 years it would have had to sit in our HISA, it would grow to a total of $9,701.72.

So again, our options are $200 after nearly half a century in an HISA, only $100 of which is profit... or we could have $9,701.72 after 48 years in a Roth IRA, $9,601.72 of which will be profit. That's over 96 times the profit because we put our money in a dedicated growth and retirement account instead of just handing it over to our bank. The difference is night and day, and that's just if we put in a single $100 deposit.

But what if, instead of only making one lump payment, we instead deposit $100 once a month, which is still an incredibly easy sacrifice for most of us?

After 48 years, we'd have contributed a total of $57,600. And our fund balance would be $1,161,908.53.

I had several large debts when I first began faithfully investing every month, but, even then, I was easily able to begin contributions of $500 per month. Utilizing methods such as the Debt Snowball, Debt Avalanche, and others at the same time helped me to eliminate a considerable amount of debt quickly, freeing up an additional $1,706.38 a month.

However, even if I had only continued to make the $500 payments to my fund in exchange for consistent returns of 10% interest, in 48 years I would have paid a total of $288,000, but my fund balance would be $5,809,542.64. Just goes to show how amazing compound interest is, and how ridiculously exponential its growth becomes the longer we can leave it running.

Of course, a lot of people aren't even in the workplace for 48 years, so the idea of making any kind of consistent contribution for that long can still seem daunting or ridiculous. However, in the next chapter, we'll cover strategies for making meaningful contributions and cash returns well into old age. How awesome would it be to take our standard retirement after around 30 years in the workplace, but still be able to easily invest $500 a month well into a comfortable retirement of 20-30 years?

Even if that doesn't interest you, I can promise you that it interests your beneficiaries.

But, No Matter How Simple It Seems...

It never hurts to have an expert advisor on hand. While Roth/TFSAs can, and do, have return rates of 10%, it isn't always easy to find one with consistent returns that high. 10% is just an easy number for the sake of examples, and we might have to make do with less. As I mentioned earlier, a return of 6-8% should be our base.

It's easy to settle for less when we can't find the best, and that's when a good advisor comes in. For more advanced strategies that we'll cover a little later, such as active-managed mutual funds or segregated funds, advisors are a must and a God-send.

But if That Seems a Bit Much

Know that a return rate of 6-8% is still enough for most people to obtain a very comfortable retirement. Just look at what 8% did to our hypothetical scenario in the last chapter. If our growth averages to around 6-7% each year, that's already fantastic, especially if we get started early. It doesn't all have to be about our retirement, either. While I put a lot of emphasis on that, since no one likes doing back-breaking work when they're elderly, growth accounts like this are also great for developing money that we can then divert into shorter-term investments. Do we want to buy that nice little fishing boat? These strategies can help us get there as well.

Just be aware that it always pays to have a strong goal or reason when making a short-term decision. Common short-term investments include saving up for a sorely-needed vacation or upgrading the tools of our trade. Other examples could be saving up enough to host a wedding our partner will never forget, or to clear off a high-interest debt as quickly as possible.

Now, For a Helpful Tool

What should we do if we aren't sure a 6-8% growth rate will be enough for us? We log into a computer. There's a free online tool sponsored by the US government made to answer exactly that kind of question. To run our financial projections, please visit www.investor.gov. Then, look at their *Financial Tools & Calculators* tab, and, finally, search for and click on their compound interest calculator. This is the one I like best, but you could just as easily run a Google search for "compound interest calculator" and find any amount of free versions online.

It's great for not only running projections on contribution plans we're seriously considering but also for having fun messing around with numbers. Since we can plug in any numbers we like for our initial investment, monthly contribution, time, and more, it's a great tool to experiment with, and we'll find that it hammers home a lot of the strategies I've shared in this book: Seeing the growth we can accumulate from very reasonable monthly contributions is another rock that should bonk us all into action.

For a more serious projection, all we need to do is estimate how much money we'll be able to contribute monthly to our growth account. Then, plug in the account's interest rate, variance, and compounding frequency. We should be able to request this information from whoever is offering us the account if we don't already have it.

Once we've plugged the relevant info in, all we need to do is input how long in years we plan to continue these contributions, and calculate. This is an easy way to discover the exciting possibilities our growth account might have. It can also tell us quickly if the growth rate is sufficient for what we're able to contribute.

Here's another fun one, which my advisor first told me about: Plugin $25 as our monthly contribution. Give a varying interest rate of 5-8%. Run the contribution from our current age to our ideal retirement age, for instance, the number of years it'd take us to reach 50 or 60 if we aren't already there. Maybe even 40 if we're feeling ambitious and thrifty at the same time.

Even people who understand how compound interest works on a rational level are always amazed to see how far we can go on so little if we just start from a young age. A 16-year-old flipping hamburgers could easily contribute $25 a month for 30 years, at a variance of 5-8%. Their total contribution is $9,000, but their fund balance would total...

I'm not going to tell you. That's your really easy homework assignment.

Hope For the Aging

To make the most of our growth, we ideally want to start investing as early as possible, between 18 and 23 years old. Or even earlier, if parents can do so in their child's name: We will discuss much more on that exciting option later on, which should be extremely interesting to both young readers, and parents who want to give their child the best possible head-start long before they're even old enough to enter the full-time workplace.

I, on the other hand, only wised up enough to start meaningful investing at the age of 36. So, yes, that $5,809,542.64 retirement projection is likely just a very pretty number on paper, since I don't feel like being in the workplace until age 84. That being said, I learned not to underestimate any possibilities in the world of investing after the first time a fund which I had an active role in selecting saw 14% growth in a single quarter. I mention this because, if you find you're in the same boat, don't despair. Earlier I said I was putting $500 a month into one of my primary growth accounts. That affordable contribution rate is still more than enough to ensure a comfortable retirement for almost anyone.

The point is that even if we start late, or are even feeling panicky as we near retirement age, late is still far better than never. While not ideal, older people can have some distinct advantages in beginning late-life investments. For example, many of them have reached their full earning potential in their company, they no longer have the expense of children living at home and may have fully paid off their mortgage. Just those three things can mean that older people often have hundreds or even thousands of dollars in available funds every month which they can begin putting into growth accounts. They'll have to pay more per month if they want to see meaningful growth for their retirement, or for leaving an inheritance to their family, but I am not exaggerating when I say this: It is NEVER too late.

Final Note on High-Interest Savings Accounts

While I don't use my HISA at all these days, and I keep it primarily because it amuses me to run the clock on how long an account can stay alive with $0.50 in it, they do have their uses.

HISA growth rates, while not spectacular, are still good enough to protect our money from the entropies of inflation, or at least to minimize the damage. This is far more than can be said of a basic savings or checking account, or the 4-gallon water jug full of change on the kitchen counter. The growth is steady, and some people feel it's more predictable than what they'd see in a growth account with higher rates, where interest is more likely to have degrees of variance. A particularly good use for HISAs is short-term spending goals separate from our long-term investments: Because I want to invest for retirement, but I also might want that nice little fishing boat one day.

However, unless we're already stinking rich, we can't expect the growth from an HISA to ever generate enough money for us to comfortably live on. What we put in is more or less what we'll get out, even if we're highly patient, motivated, and disciplined in regular contributions.

Our most financially viable plan by far is to use our HISA only as a temporary holding area for our money until we find a better place to send it. Think of our HISA like the nexus of a railway, like Grand Central Terminal. It's a great place to put our money until we've figured out how to split it between our various growth accounts. Even when we are looking at short-term goals like the fishing boat, talk to an advisor about a short-term fund with no penalties for early withdrawal. As soon as we find one, it's time to take that HISA balance back down to $0.50.

The only other recommendation I can make for an HISA is to use it as a growth option once all better choices have been maxed out, or become non-viable: If contributing an extra $1,000 into our Roth/TFSA would put us over the annual contribution cap and incur extra fees, we're probably better off putting it into our HISA instead. Or, if our advisor lets us know that a growth fund is in serious peril, we might want to pull it out and put it in holding in the HISA until they can find us a more secure option: Minimal growth is better than none in the meantime. Even then, we might be better off looking towards other options not discussed in this book, such as stocks, crypto, small-business startups, or precious metals.

All in all, the HISA has its place. It's a great first pick until we know how to divvy up our contributions, and it's a great last pick for any money we may have leftover after that.

However, at no point is it the place for us to grow long-term savings, even when we're young. It's the last resort. Feeling like we need to make this account a high priority for savings is just part of the hierarchical model of thinking which we must smash, or train ourselves to reverse.

6

ROTH IRA TRUMPS TRADITIONAL IRA:

PAYING THE EXTRA TAX NOW CAN SAVE A TON OF TAX LATER

B ack in Chapter 1, we started touching on how Roth/TFSAs should be a higher priority than traditional IRA/RRSPs. In Chapter 4, we elaborated on this a little more and, in both Chapters 4 and 5, we began digging into the deliciousness of the math behind the potential growth rates of these accounts.

Now, as promised, we're going to dive into Roth/TFSAs, and explain how we can manage them properly at every stage of life. Saddle up.

Step 4: Open Your Roth IRA or Tax-Free Savings Account First.

Before we go further, I think it'll help if I first explain what a basic IRA is, as compared to its Canadian counterpart, the basic RRSP.

At the time of this writing, the biggest difference we need to bear in mind is that a normal IRA only allows us to contribute $6,000 into our account each year. Once the owner of the account turns 50 years old, this limit increases to $7,000 a year.

By contrast, the RRSP allows 18% of a Canadian's annual income to be deposited each year instead but also has a hard upper limit. In 2021, this limit is a rather impressive $27,830 per year, almost 4x the maximum allowable in an American IRA.

For this reason, many people in the US are calling for banking reforms to more closely mirror the Canadian model. Should you be interested in this, the best option is to contact your local or state representative and petition for a similar change, as it is a huge advantage for Canadian investors. However, even if those changes are distant or not forthcoming, similar investment strategies can still be used to maximize the potential of the IRA's annual $6,000 contribution.

Compared to an HISA, IRA/RRSPs can seem like quite attractive options. That said, if we still remember the rough road of Roy and Annie, we'll also remember that just because an option seems great, that doesn't mean it's the one we should prioritize. I need to stress this, since too often a young person will learn the truth about HISAs only to settle for an option that isn't necessarily a whole lot better, and find themselves the target of constant adverts and banking pressures: A promise the adverts love to make is that their options will help the account holder reach certain tax-advantages, such as reducing short-term tax or even pushing them down to a lower tax bracket.

This one kid I knew figured out the inefficacy of HISAs while he was still in high school, but he also refused to look beyond the IRA/RRSP options. I don't know why a kid spraying disinfectant into rental shoes at a bowling alley felt such a strong need to knock himself down by one tax bracket rather than frantically scrambling up toward the next one,—although he did mention the hair color and cup-size of the bank teller he was working with multiple times—but I also don't stand in severe judgment of those who demonstrate ambitious economic prerogatives early in life.

The Pros and Cons

Possibly the biggest disadvantage of the US investment model is that the maximum contribution to a traditional IRA is not stackable with the maximum contribution to a Roth IRA: We can either contribute the full amount to an IRA or Roth IRA, or we can contribute a portion to each one not exceeding the maximum, but we cannot contribute the full amount to both.

Earlier, I mentioned how a Canadian TFSA can only have a max of $6,000 put into it each year, while an IRA or Roth IRA can have $6,000 at first, which then rises to $7,000 when the account holder turns 50. In isolation, this makes the US model look better, but, in reality, Canada in 2021 has a much easier strategy because its accounts are stackable, which means a Canadian investor can sink a total of $33,380 into tax-deferred or tax-free growth accounts each year: $27,830 into their RRSP, and $6,000 into their TFSA.

The US investor, meanwhile, must choose between $6-7,000 in a Roth IRA, $6-7,000 in a traditional IRA, or a $6-7,000 split between both. While the difference between the two models isn't that huge when we're low-income, it does mean that, once we're looking to break past a certain growth threshold, the US investor will have little choice but to move on to 401(k)s or invest in the risky world of stock markets if they want an even more comfortable retirement.

Canadian investors, if they're clever, may go through their entire working lives and never need to invest in much more than their TFSA and RRSP. Even with the back-end taxes that plague RRSPs, combined with a good TFSA the total growth would still be more than enough to live comfortably for a long time by the time the investor hits retirement age.

As if that weren't enough, TFSAs offer a little more leeway in the way Canadians make their contributions. For example, if we could put in $6,000 in our first year, but couldn't afford to put in anything the next year, we could contribute up to $12,000 in the year after that. In comparison, an IRA, or even a Roth IRA, doesn't care if we missed a year. If we cannot contribute the maximum amount each year, and miss out on potential growth because of it, tough beans.

There's even a little trick Canadians can use right now if they turned 18 in or before 2009, the year when the TFSA was first implemented: They can backdate their contributions back to that year. (TFSAs can only be purchased by adults over the age of 18.)

What do I mean by that? I mean that the maximum contribution isn't just $6,000. It's $6,000 plus the maximum TFSA value of every preceding year going back to 2009. So, if we've never contributed to a TFSA before 2021, we could kickstart our growth into a brand new one with an impressive initial investment of $75,500 if we have that available. (It's noteworthy that the contribution cap has varied in previous years, i.e., some years allowed only $5,000 while other years allowed up to $10,000. The current total of $75,500 is the sum of each of the total allowable contributions from all previous years: If the sum was based on only $6,000 for each previous year, the total allowable in 2021 would only be $72,000.)

This is an amazing feature for those who start investing late, particularly those who have been ineffectually saving large amounts of money in basic bank accounts or HISAs. Even if we're only beginning our savings journey well into adulthood, we won't be too badly punished for tardiness thanks to that backdating feature. An absolute blessing for those who need more time, while those who were too young to backdate very far—say a kid who turned 19 or 20 in 2009—still had plenty of time to build up contributions in the slow and steady way instead. Likewise, young people who recently turned 18 cannot backdate contributions, but this is less of a problem as they have their entire adult life ahead of them.

If I'm being totally honest, if you live in Canada, you're going to have a relatively easy time getting your savings off the starting blocks compared to someone trying to grow investments in the USA, so don't ever take that for granted. However, it is also noteworthy that Canadian youth of today are just as plagued by debt and uncertainty as American kids, and for the exact same reason: These strategies are not taught in school.

By contrast, those in the US of A who want to prepare for a secure retirement must start young, scrappy, and hungry if they don't want to waste their shot.

Understanding the Roth IRA and Tax-Free Savings Accounts

One of the most important things to remember about Roth/TFSAs is that we can withdraw the money we put in it at any time, for any reason we like, and, unlike an HISA, we won't be charged a penalty. We won't even be taxed retroactively. This means the money we put in is still easily accessible if an emergency comes up and we suddenly need it for food, hospitalization, or something else.

Fees may start to be charged once we withdraw the money we grew, however. The only part that's truly liquid is the money we put in ourselves. Any interest we earn in those accounts can have a charge associated with the withdrawal. However, unlike an IRA/RRSP, our withdrawals are never taxable even in these circumstances.

Roth/TFSAs are thus great tax-shelters, allowing us to effectively make powerful investments without experiencing the massive tax hits that so often come with trying to grow our wealth. When contributing to these accounts, we'll typically have a choice of assets to put the money in. A financial advisor will say great growth potential, high turnover, or large dividends are signs of a great asset, but as long as the account we choose has a high return rate, we'll generally be okay.

We also don't have to worry about overkill with our growth, as we can typically transfer our account to a beneficiary, meaning we can leave all the money we accumulated to a loved one in our will.

The reason Roth/TFSAs are referred to as after-tax accounts is not what people often mistakenly think: That the contributions themselves are subject to a front-end tax when initially paid, but the remainder can then grow-tax free up til and including withdrawal. That is a common misconception that even I failed to realize at first, which is why—along with the seemingly ridiculous $6,000 contribution cap—I once thought Roth/TFSAs were pointless.

Lately, I've begun to suspect that this is exactly what banks and the government wanted me to think.

The actual reason they are called after-tax accounts relates to our income tax. Roth/TFSAs cannot be used for income tax deductions, which is another reason that IRA/RRSPs initially sound so good: They reduce the amount of income tax we pay each year, and the full amount contributed then grows tax-free. Which sounds fantastic until we try to, you know, withdraw and use it.

So, when we contribute to a Roth/TFSA our taxable income for the year remains the same, and we pay the same amount of income tax. That is why the accounts can exist and grow tax-free: The money in them was already taxed years ago.

Why Are Roth IRAs and TFSAs Underrated, and Why Is This Backwards?

There are a few reasons why this idea is taking so long to catch on, but most of them come down to advertising. Aside from that, the biggest reason why Roth/TFSAs get ignored is that we can't contribute any money into them that hasn't already been taxed, and most people who think "in the now" will do just about anything to maximize that year's income tax return or pay less tax. With an IRA/RRSP, as mentioned earlier, we can theoretically knock ourselves down into a lower tax bracket just by making our annual contribution into them, meaning we can lower the tax we get hit with in the short term.

A fact of life is that many families need $100,000 a year just to survive in modern times, but don't necessarily have a lot of income to meet that mark comfortably. Life has gotten better in many ways, but that doesn't mean we're living in luxury yet.

When a family is not especially rich, but one year finds that they have just barely edged into a higher tax bracket by a few dollars, they might try to preserve the value of those extra few dollars as best they can by tucking them into an IRA/RRSP, in the hopes that this will help make ends meet later on. If we want or need bigger tax returns in the short term, it can be difficult to choose anything besides a traditional IRA/RRSP. This can then lead to contribution habits and an unwillingness to change as people stick with what is most familiar to them, regardless of what is best for them in the long run.

Thanks to emotional complications getting the better of us, the idea of less tax right now—or a nice, fat tax return—is always tempting. It's a way of appealing to our want for instant gratification while still looking like we're being responsible on the surface. Just put our money into a normal IRA/RRSP, and the tax gets deferred off into the sunset. Out of sight and mind.

In contrast, with the Roth/TFSA, we always have to deal with the full brunt of the "here and now" taxman. However, there's a reason I recommend them so strongly, despite coming from a working-class family that could have always stood to benefit from paying less immediate tax.

The reason is this: Paying a little extra tax now can save you a heck of a lot of extra tax later. In the US, tax brackets currently vary from 10-37%. In Canada, the range goes from 15-33%. On top of that, in both countries, the tax rate can jump to 40% when factoring in supplemental income and capital gains.

All that being understood, the very nature of growth accounts means being willing to lose around 20-40% of the money we have now. And we willingly do this, because that amount is absolutely nothing when compared to losing 20-40% of a nest egg we spent 30 years or more growing at a compounding interest rate of 8-10%.

To draw from one of our earlier examples, 20-40% of $100 is only $20-$40. Not a huge loss, and realistically, there's a good chance we're only going to lose $20 or $30 from that hundred, not $40, although 40% will be most frequently mentioned as a worst-case scenario... which a whole lot of real people are currently living in.

So, we'd lose maybe $30 of tax before we contribute $100 to a Roth/TFSA. That stings a little bit.

Now imagine, instead of the Roth/TFSA, we instead withdraw from a traditional IRA/RRSP. Using the example from the last chapter, we put in our $100 without tax, enjoy the tax break for that year, and over the next 48 years it grows into a lovely $9,701.72. We try to withdraw it, the withdrawal tax kicks in, and now instead of losing 20-40% of $100, we're losing 20-40% of $9,701.72.

I ask you, would you rather lose a maximum of $40 in tax now, or anywhere from $1,940.35 to $3,880.69 in tax later? (For the record, my editor keeps telling me to round off my figures, but the thought of my audiobook narrator having to repeatedly recite these exact figures in a sound booth while not letting *any* frustration creep into their voice is amusing to me. If we can't have fun, what is all the money in the world really worth?)

Repeat that cost for each time we prioritize a traditional IRA/RRSP over contributions to a Roth/TFSA. For instance, if we want to withdraw $60,000 from a traditional IRA/RRSP, we'd need to withdraw $100,000, since $40,000 of that $100,000 would disappear into the netherworld of tax. That's a heck of a lot of money to lose after a lifetime of hard labor went into earning it, and it's probably even frustrating if you've spent your life as a lazy worthless Commie freeloader or as a blue-haired equity-driven social justice activist. Even if we're being more lenient and saying we're getting taxed 20%, rather than 40% like Roy and Annie, we'd still be losing tens of thousands of dollars to tax at a time when there's probably not a lot of income incoming anymore.

I hope I've made my point. Even if we can benefit from having an immediate tax reduction, I must stress that if we can afford to rather cut corners on non-essentials somewhere—*anywhere* —to put money into a Roth/TFSA first, that's what we should do. If most of our contributions are sitting in a traditional IRA/RRSP, we're going to get the same shock Roy and Annie did. (And even if we are now prepared for it, I still can't see how that back-end tax is something that anyone would eagerly look forward to.) It's important to internalize that even if we're in a fairly low tax bracket now, withdrawals from an IRA/RRSP later in life are often given the full tax rate of over 40%. Realistically, our choice isn't between saving $40 now or almost $4,000 later. (There, I rounded for once. Happy now, Narrators Union?) If our current income is truly the lowest of the low, the choice might even be a $10 to $15 loss on our $100 investment now... or a $4,000 loss later. When we consider that, as well as the fact that IRA/RRSP withdrawals are more likely to be made at a time when we no longer have the same peak level of income to offset the losses, it really is no contest as to which type of account we should contribute to first.

It's a huge problem that, when people do have extra money to save, aggressive advertising means they're often putting it into an IRA/RRSP. Particularly in Canada, for example, the RRSP's large contribution limit is a boon to the savvy, but it's also a trap for the desperate. A surprising amount of people, desperate to make more money for later in life, think that the way to save is to get more raises, earn bigger salaries, work longer hours, and therefore make bigger contributions into their RRSP, with the tax reductions and higher tax returns being the cherry on top that clinches it.

As mentioned earlier, contributing as much money as possible into the IRA/RRSP often becomes a habit for those who don't have a lot of financial curiosity, leading to a situation where people will max it out year after year, leaving themselves barely anything for what will keep them well-off later in life: Their Roth/TFSAs. The hungrier they are, the more they feed the IRA/RRSP, and the more they will eventually find themselves owing to the most-patient-of-all-foes, the taxman.

Again, we go back to our example of the couple who paid their mortgage off over the entire 30-year amortization period. They didn't even need to maximize their contributions to a Roth/TFSA, let alone a maxed-out IRA or hungry, hungry RRSP. They paid $442.70 a month for 30 years, and they were sitting pretty darn pretty just from that.

Other Advantages of Roth IRAs and TFSAs

Aside from losing us far less money in the future, Roths/TFSAs have several other distinct advantages over their traditional counterparts.

For instance, a traditional IRA/RRSP can only be used until we turn 71 years old. Then, like a scene out of *Logan's Run*, the government decides we've officially become non-contributing old farts and hand us an ultimatum. Like all ultimatums, it has two outcomes, neither of which are that great:

1. Withdraw all our money, stopping its growth cold, and just hope there's still enough leftovers after the taxman takes his hefty bite out of it. And, just for the

record, this is the choice which the government will make for us if we don't make our own choice in time.

2. Convert our account into a Registered Retirement Income Fund (RRIF) in Canada, or a variety of US equivalents. Although these still allow growth, this account type mandates that we withdraw a minimum percentage each year, even if it's far more than we need. They also don't allow us to make contributions, so hopefully, we've budgeted how many years we plan to live as well as we budgeted our cash.

On the flip side, a Roth/TFSA does not have any restrictions like this. We can use it freely until the day we die. A common choice for many Canadians who had to convert their RRSP into an RRIF is to put the excess of their forced withdrawals into a TFSA. Sadly, by that time they're over the age of 71, and it's way too late to see a lot of meaningful growth from even the best TFSAs. But it still beats the alternative.

The relative flexibility of Roth/TFSAs in our withdrawals is important, as the 71-year age limit on traditional growth accounts makes a rather dangerous assumption, namely that our bucket is about to be kicked. I understand that the blue-haired people recently decreed it racist to make jokes about certain cultures setting their elderly populace adrift on an ice flow, but I can't get that image out of my head every time I think about the IRA/RRSP age limit and mandatory minimum withdrawals. (Also, I'm too damn old to care what the blue-haired people designate as racist anymore, because I honestly can't keep up with it all, and, full disclosure, I never actually watched the entirety of *Logan's Run*. I got the gist: *Blade Runner* is better.)

There's another dangerous assumption that comes with the 71-year age limit: That we've already retired. This isn't necessarily the case for lower-income geriatrics, who often have to work full-time as mechanics, consultants, or more to get by, to say nothing of those who are still getting up at 5 a.m. to milk cows and thresh corn on the family farm. Especially if they've been using an inferior growth account such as an IRA/RRSP. People who sell traditional IRA/RRSPs typically suggest that, by the time we make our withdrawals, our marginal tax will be lower, implying that maybe we won't be hit as hard as our earlier calculations suggested.

The people who sell the IRA/RRSPs may even suggest that federal tax rates across the board may have lowered nationwide by the time we retire. Sometimes they even manage to say it with a straight face.

While people do tend to be in a lower tax bracket as they ease into retirement by often having a smaller income stream than when they were in their prime, it doesn't change the fact that traditional growth accounts will still apply tax to every withdrawal we make. And, again, withdrawals from these traditional accounts become compulsory once we're 71, even when we're forced by circumstance to still be working full-time, sitting in a higher tax bracket in our old age because of misfortunes earlier

YOU CAN'T HAVE MY MONEY! | 99

in life. And, of course, Heaven help us if we run into the same issue as Roy and Annie, where our withdrawal is also counted as supplemental income, giving us the highest tax rate of all.

Oh, and one more thing: Because that withdrawal counts as income, it is used by the Canadian government as an excuse to claw back Old Age Security (OAS) entitlements. Really makes the seniors feel validated after decades of, you know, building the country and whatnot.

So, that's one advantage Roth/TFSAs have over traditional accounts. Another advantage is that, unlike traditional accounts, they also allow us to look beyond our bank, just like we should be doing. We are typically able to direct the way we fund our contributions into Roth/TFSAs. If we have an advisor on board, then we truly do have the big picture in mind. We are in a much better position to make advantageous decisions, allowing us to seek better deals if we feel our initial investments aren't paying off. In contrast, a traditional account is more or less bound to the bank and the investments it is interested in, limiting our ability to easily navigate into a better spot if we aren't happy with our current growth.

How Much Does It Pay to Have an Advisor?

Simply put, it pays a heck of a lot. Roth/TFSAs are a great choice we can make for long-term growth, but there does come a point when a traditional IRA/RRSP can become useful. They are generally most valuable for those who already earn a higher-than-average income or have already established sufficient retirement security. Being able to see where this fine line exists between unnecessary expense and prudent investing is the financial advisor's specialty.

Even if we aren't high-income or already retirement-protected, we can still benefit from an advisor. Not everyone is great at math, so having someone look over the money we're contributing can be a lifesaver. For example, the annual contribution limits on Roth/TFSAs don't outright block us from accidentally going over: If we're not careful, we can contribute as much as we want, and may not even know it. However, if we bypass the hard limit, we will experience much slower growth as penalties start to kick in, such as a monthly deduction made off our account's balance every month, or even having our account's tax-exemption waived... at which point we're basically sitting on an IRA/RRSP with a less impressive annual limit. Accidentally surpassing that is something we want to avoid at all costs. Otherwise, we've negated the entire purpose of an after-tax account. Having a trained, qualified professional look after our investments is not a weakness. It's wise to seek guidance from the experts when we find ourselves out of our depth.

True story, I once got a phone call from local police officers, not because I was in trouble, but because they had encountered stray cows on the highway outside of town and had no idea how to get rid of them. Let's just say that I had to arrange for several hours of mid-shift coverage for my non-ranch job, and dust off the cowboy boots and cattle cane which had become nostalgia pieces by that point in my life.

All over the country, police commissioners are installing special red phones to be used only in the event of cow-related crises: "I need somebody who can crack these cloven-hoofed wiseguys, McMann! *Get me Finnegan!*"

Advisors are also all but a necessity for those who want the benefits of active-managed funds, as we'll discuss in Chapter 7. The funds we put into a Roth/TFSA don't have to just sit there. They can be used for other things, namely funds beyond our own bank. In the hands of an accredited financial advisor,—or even a life agent, as we will also discuss later—the money in our Roth/TFSA can become carefully managed funds, which go by different regional names. In the US, they are less clearly defined and more confusing nationally, and may require a little digging to find at all: Again, this is why advisor's may be needed. In some regions, these managed funds are known as Separate Accounts or simply managed mutual funds. However, in other regions the name Separate Account refers to a far more cost-prohibitive method requiring a minimum investment of $100,000, making it all but useless to a lower-to-middle income investor. In Canada, the funds are a much-more developed tool and referred to exclusively as Segregated Funds.

My opinion, and heartfelt recommendation, is that this is another issue that should be brought to US state representatives and fund managers. The streamlined Canadian model of Segregated Funds is one of the fastest-growing investment alternatives to stocks and mutual funds. Their popularity stems from both the earning potential and the additional investment security provided by fund managers.

Of course, that higher reward isn't without risk, and our growth becomes a lot more vulnerable to the market hills and valleys when it's going into a segregated fund. That 14% quarterly growth I experienced definitely wasn't the perpetual norm, and many readers may prefer sticking with 7-10% growth instead, as that is already more than enough for those starting young, while also being consistent with their risk tolerance. However, having an advisor minimizes the risk and can even prevent serious losses that we'd almost certainly run into if we were to attempt high-risk strategies on our own. Why? Because the majority of us have day-jobs beyond round-the-clock monitoring of our investments' market trends. We don't have time to be looking two quarters down the road to project future fund values. Even if we're well on our way to becoming professional investors, we still benefit from the mentorship of an advisor.

Advisors also play a key role for investors who start late. Naturally, the later we start, the fewer doubling periods our money will go through before retirement. We all know by now how big an impact starting even 12 years later can have on your ability to enjoy tax-free growth, thanks to our mortgage illustration from Chapter 4. A good many Americans end up kicking themselves and wishing they were taught about Roth IRAs in school. A great many more end up going their whole lives without even knowing what a Roth IRA is. All this, despite living in an age where it is now more important than ever for all young people in America, especially those from lower-income families, to know about such simple investment tips.

In any case, those who start their investment journey late have to work extremely hard to adequately make up for lost time, which can mean opening up a 401(k) account as a supplement. Advisors are invaluable in this situation, as they can help us run the numbers and double-check the math to help us decide where we should focus our contributions. Unless we have enough money to max out both our Roth IRA and 401(k), it pays to have an advisor to help optimize our investing.

When we have the choice between two or more growth investment platforms, precisely where we should focus our contributions can fluctuate a lot depending on market conditions, so we'll need someone with inside knowledge or understanding of the system to accurately tell whether our 401(k) or Roth IRA will save us the most in tax and give us the most growth in return for our contributions. This can save us a great deal of time and stress. Although starting early on a Roth IRA will save us that same time and stress for much less cost and effort, it would be imprudent of me to suggest that everyone reading this book invested in a DeLorean.

Learning A Little More About 401(k)s

Normally, a 401(k) is given not through an institution or advisor, but rather through an employer. For those who feel an advisor isn't necessary to help them run their 401(k) account, please note that whether or not we should prioritize it over our Roth IRA can vary according to all sorts of trends. In the US, even politics can determine the viability of one account over the other, and to make a 401(k) consistently work for us, we must be willing to change our plans completely every few years as economic policies change with each administration. While we tend to give in to our biases when looking at political matters, there is never a more important time to shut off the emotion and turn to the economy with a purely analytical eye. If nothing else, we need to be able to pivot our financial planning on short notice, dependant not so much on who's leading the country, but rather the economic policies most likely to be legislated during that administrative term, at both the state and federal level.

For example, in 2012, during President Barack Obama's second term, many experts were led to believe, quite reasonably in the wake of a crippling economic crisis, that income tax rates would continue to rise until they were on the same level as most of Europe's, and they made their investment choices accordingly. Deferring tax was considered to be an especially bad idea compared to just eating it and investing in a Roth IRA.

However, these same experts saw their projections change drastically when 2017 rolled around and President Donald Trump enacted the Tax Cuts and Job Act, which gave substantial tax breaks to 80% of American workers as well as small businesses. The median household income saw an average increase of $5,000 nationwide. This meant people had a greater ability to make meaningful contributions to growth investments, and gave smaller businesses more room to expand and hire additional employees. While the Roth IRA was still arguably the better option, the distinction was not so clear as it had been 5 years earlier. Even those who were just entering into retirement at this time found they weren't bitten as badly by having chosen traditional accounts.

The lower taxes also meant people were more comfortable with prioritizing Roth IRAs since being limited to contributing only with after-tax income suddenly didn't feel like such a big hit to blue-collar workers all over the US.

However, at the time of this writing during the Biden administration, serious consideration is being given to repealing this act, in which case income tax rates will likely return to levels seen a decade earlier. If this happens, traditional IRAs are likely to see a surge in popularity once more, as they will seem more attractive on a surface level. A consistent trend is that people experiencing rising tax rates will want to defer or reduce their income tax payments whenever possible, in the hope that future legislation enacted closer to their planned retirement drops the tax rate back down again. Long-term plans are often abandoned during times of seeming crisis. It takes courage and a lot of planning to hold fast to the best course of retirement investing when times are lean. Especially when our banks are still telling us how much tax deductions we can claim *right now* by taking out an IRA with them. That gets tempting.

Since our employer often has to match a percentage of what we contribute into a 401(k), this growth account generates more value for us compared to the money we put into it vs a traditional IRA, making it more viable as a way to reduce the impact of immediate tax on us now, as the larger tax later won't hurt so much.

There also exists, of course, the Roth 401(k) for those who still prefer to be taxed more now in exchange for being taxed much less later. However, which version of 401(k) we should focus on isn't as clear-cut as which version of IRA we should prioritize.

When deciding how to contribute to a traditional 401(k), it also pays to think about what state we're living in, and whether or not we want our retirement to be in that same state. This is because not all states have the same tax rates on income, so while a traditional 401(k) may seem better in one state, a Roth 401(k) would be much better in another. Whether we move from a state with low-income tax to one with high, or high to low, we need to anticipate our investment strategies changing a bit.

In cases where we expect our tax rate to be low now, but much higher towards retirement, the Roth 401(k) is the way to go. In cases where our rate is currently high, but we know for a fact it'll be much lower once we retire, the regular 401(k) can work well.

The First Great American Equalizer: The Roth 401(k)

As a rule of thumb, I still say eating the tax now is worth not having to worry about being taxed later. If we don't have an advisor with us to crunch the numbers and see whether a traditional or Roth 401(k) will be better for you, go with the Roth.

But what if we now have to choose between a Roth 401(k) and a Roth IRA? If we don't have the money to maximize contributions to both, this can be an agonizing decision.

Which is better depends on a few factors. However, in many ways, the Roth 401(k) is one of the biggest advantages for someone in the US, acting as a better IRA while still having some of the perks of a traditional 401(k).

While a Roth IRA can only accept $6,000-7,000 in contributions each year, a Roth 401(k) can accept $19,500 each year, with some allowances for catch-up contributions. While it's never ideal to start late, this is one of the better ways to catch up once we've maxed out our Roth IRA.

An important question to consider is this: Does our employer support Roth 401(k)s? Do they match a percentage of our contributions into them, like they would for a traditional 401(k)? If so, then the Roth 401(k) can seem more appealing. Are we extremely high in income? If we can max out our Roth 401(k)'s contribution limit, even after tax, that's another point in its favor. However, employers won't normally match us all the way on that unless our salary is already in the high-income range. Even so, we can still contribute a respectable amount every year.

Another point in the Roth 401(k)'s favor is that, unlike the Roth IRA, it doesn't have an income limit. Each year the Roth IRA is either restricted, or outright closed, to those earning above a certain limit, such as more than $125,000-140,000 each year after modifications and adjustments. This limit is higher for those who are married. In a country where the average person earns between $50,000 and $75,000 a year, this limit rarely comes up, but it is something that high-income earners must factor into their retirement planning as well. Again, the strategies in this book are designed to be utilized by anyone who wants to try a new method, regardless of location, age, education, or income level. My goal is for this book to be a unification for every investor: No matter what amount of money or income we start with, we can all follow the same basic steps to success or greater success.

Unlike a Roth IRA, the Roth 401(k) doesn't let us take our money back out very easily when we aren't retired. If we're already bringing in a high enough income for the Roth 401(k) to be warranted, it's less likely that we'd need to make a sudden withdrawal from it anyway, but, as always, there will be exceptions. Speaking from personal experience, my highest annual earnings put me into the income range where a Roth 401(k) was a better option. However, that was also the time of my life when my monthly expenses hit an all-time high, which meant that the smartest move for me was the options with greater liquidity. I cannot emphasize it enough: Your personal and financial circumstances are as unique as your fingerprints. Any plan you make must be personalized, and that is why an advisor will almost always be your best option.

Another point against the Roth 401(k) is that, like a traditional IRA/RRSP, we can't keep it open forever. At the age of 72, we must withdraw. Fortunately, this account type is more flexible than the traditional ones, because we don't need to withdraw if we're still in the workplace, and the withdrawals we do make can be rolled right over into a Roth IRA with little fuss.

Overall, the Roth 401(k) is less flexible, but it can be a great equalizer for US investors who may be feeling frustrated, especially when they have learned the advantages of their Canadian counterparts. Since a Roth 401(k) has some distinct advantages over an RRSP in any case, America still has a lot to cheer about.

Before we move on, here are some important tips on using 401(k)s and Roth IRAs together:

1. If our income qualifies as too high for a Roth IRA,

contributing into a traditional 401(k) first can help, since the normal 401(k) contribution happens before tax, while the Roth IRA checks our income after-tax.

2. If our 401(k) is already maxed, we can instead place the contribution into a traditional IRA, then roll it into a Roth IRA. However, be aware that this will come with a penalty since we'll be moving deferred-tax money into an after-tax account. Think of this penalty as a retroactive tax.

3. If we can contribute to both the 401(k) and the Roth IRA fully without penalties, and we're using a Roth 401(k) instead of a traditional one, we could instead look at the investment fees, and focus on the one that charges us the least for what we put into it. 1% is what I consider too high, 0.5% is just fine.

4. Social Security benefits can, and will, be taxed if our income is seen as high enough. Withdrawals from a 401(k) may be read as income, but withdrawals from a Roth IRA won't. It still pays to maximize contributions to our Roth IRA each year if we can.

5. Building up a strong Roth 401(k) is a great way to have income to roll over into our Roth IRA later, allowing it to continue growing faster for longer as we hit the impressive milestone of 70+ years old.

The Second Great American Equalizer: Your Child's Roth IRA

Saddle up, America, because we're about to delve into possibly the greatest investing advantage exclusive to the US of A. As we discussed earlier, Canadians who start investing later in life can backdate TFSA contributions back to 2009, but American investors do not have that luxury. They must start young, ideally by the time they're 18.

But here's where the story changes. In the US we can, as parents, decide that our kid can start even earlier than that: Roth IRAs can be purchased for children by their parents.

There are a few rules to this, though:

1. Our child must be earning some form of verifiable income. This can include babysitting, farm and ranch work, dog-walking, yard work or landscaping, newspaper delivery, washing cars, fast-food and retail jobs, or even lifeguarding and first aid if they qualify.

2. The child cannot contribute more to their Roth IRA than their total earnings. This is to prevent parents from fraudulently using their children to own multiple Roth IRAs.

3. The allowance that we give to our kids doesn't count as income for their IRA. The upper limit for our child's Roth IRA still caps at $6,000 per year, but only if they are earning at least that amount from an actual job.

However, as we've demonstrated repeatedly, these contribution caps are barely an impediment, especially for young investors. Contributions of only a few thousand dollars a year at this age could easily translate into millions of dollars by the time our kid is ready to retire, even if this Roth IRA is the only investing tool they ever use.

For instance, if we have a 15-year-old daughter, Li'l Sue, who starts investing only $500 a year—around $41.67 a month—into a Roth IRA with an average 8% growth rate, by the time she reaches 70 years old, she'd have a tax-free $427,367.20 waiting for her. Not bad considering that she only contributed $27,500 over 55 years.

More lucratively, let's say she contributes $1,000 a year. That's still only 88.33 a month, with a total lifetime contribution of $55,000. She'd have $854,631.84 by age 70.

Now imagine she decides to go big and contribute $3,000 a year. That's still only $250 a month, for a lifetime total of $165,000.

By age 70, she'd have $2,563,998.07.

Contributions of this level would be very manageable even just from utilizing the concepts in this book when combined with a modicum of self-discipline.

The low income the girl would generally earn during her teen years isn't as much of a drawback as we might expect, for three reasons:

4. Because her tax rate is either very low or absolute zero, almost all her earnings can go directly into her Roth IRA, although it's still wise for us to keep a logbook somewhere with all of her income truthfully recorded in case the IRS wants to ask questions later. The primacy of a paper trail is something we should all aspire to throughout our lives, and teach to our kids.

5. What Li'l Sue puts into her Roth IRA, we can match. If she puts in $500 in a given year, we can put $500 on top of that in that same year as well. This total still can't exceed their income for the year or the annual $6,000 maximum: She would need to have earned a total of $1,000 that year for us to add our $500, and our matching funds cannot exceed $3,000—half of the annual cap—if she earns $6,000 or more.

6. She can be free to enjoy some of her earnings on games, movies, food, and social events while still dutifully setting a percentage aside for her future. It can be difficult to convince our child to think about old age. It's hard enough to even get adults to do that, but if we show them the value of compound interest, it gets easier: Hundreds of dollars can become hundreds of thousands, and thousands of dollars can become millions. If she's motivated enough to consistently earn an income, she'll be motivated enough to spare some of it for later.

7. If Li'l Sue can get in the habit of putting away an average of $16 a day, she can look forward to becoming a tax-free millionaire.

Final Notes

When we can afford to, diversifying between our Roth/TFSA along with either a traditional IRA/RRSP or 401(k) is a fantastic idea. For all the grief I give the more traditional methods, they do have the one big perk of having protection against insolvency. It's unlikely we'd need to file for bankruptcy when we've eliminated all our high-interest debts, but knowing we have a nest egg that'll stick by us even if we lose everything else can feel reassuring, even if it means having to eat extra tax later in life.

However, the chances of that worst-case scenario are tiny compared to our chances of reaching retirement and needing to make a withdrawal. When in doubt, or without an advisor to enhance our insight with situational nuances, it's smart to always focus on our Roth/TFSA first, kind of like a reverse Debt Snowball: Maxing out our growth accounts with the smallest cap first. It doesn't hurt that they tend to have some of the best rates of return, either. When making forced withdrawals from traditional accounts later in life, always place a portion of those withdrawals straight back into our Roth/TFSA, as this will help us keep it growing even once we're technically no longer earning an income. We might alternatively decide to withdraw from our traditional accounts first before even touching the contents of our Roth/TFSA, which again is made easier by the mandatory withdrawal age.

This is a great way to keep ourselves comfortable as we enter into our seventies: Keep our Roth/TFSA going and growing for as long as we can. We always benefit from having something in it, and never benefit from leaving it low or empty.

From now on, I would recommend this type of account as the first one we contribute to, and the last one we withdraw from once we retire. However, no matter how we go about using our accounts, remember we'll always benefit from an advisor: Their job is to help protect our gains and maximize our earnings.

Be aware of differences from state to state, and how they can impact the way and rates at which we're taxed. This can influence whether it's better to focus on our Roth IRA or a traditional 401(k), though, as always, go for the Roth first if we're in doubt. For those with higher income, never forget we can open a Roth 401(k) too, allowing us to do a "double-Roth," investing large amounts of our money into future growth. The 401(k) is the best friend not only of the late starter, but also of high-income earners in general: They can frequently use it, have their employers match part of it, and then use the fact that their after-tax income is technically lower now to fill up their Roth IRA without penalty.

With a little bit of careful management like this, we can safeguard our future, and teach our kids to do the same.

7

PULLING THE OL' SWITCHEROO:

HOW INVESTING IN AN ACTIVE-MANAGED MUTUAL FUND OR SEGREGATED FUND CAN PROTECT YOUR MONEY BETTER THAN REGULAR MUTUAL FUNDS

W hen handling a Roth/TFSA, we might notice many of our contributions are effectively going into mutual funds. This is typically sufficient to achieve the gains of 6-8% we've already waxed lyrical on, provided this is the return rate we were promised would be most likely.

As such, this is a passive, comfortable form of growth. However, there is an advantage to shifting our Roth/TFSA contributions into actively managed segregated funds. Although it might seem a little pricier to the untrained eye, there are key advantages to consider, such as better protection of our money and its overall earnings.

This brings us to...

Step 5: Put an Active-Managed Mutual Fund Into Your Roth IRA, or put an Insurance-Based Segregated Fund Into Your TFSA.

Once we've looked beyond our bank, embraced the concept of OPM, learned the Rule of 72, and opened our Roth/TFSA first, we'll find ourselves in a great position to dip our toes into Step 5: Getting into active-managed funds.

Before we jump in though, it's important we ask a few questions.

What Is a Mutual Fund?

Stacy's story already covered the basics, but let's dig a little deeper. Multiple investors coming together and pooling their funds for a group of managers to handle means that a mutual fund isn't just an investment. It's a company. Everyone pooling money together would be the shareholders. The chief fund manager or financial advisor would effectively be the CEO. The chief manager could then hire under-managers and financial analysts as employees, but this isn't always the case. The first modern mutual fund was launched in the US in 1924, but remained obscure until they achieved extreme gains for their shareholders in the 1980s and 90s. In large part, they survived and grew as they could survive massive market crashes, like the Great Depression, whereas more volatile, close-ended funds often had to shut down.

Today, active-managed mutual funds exist but are relatively overlooked in favor of the passive model. This is because active-managed funds are difficult to run properly without a skilled team of analysts, researchers, or economists, which drives up their costs. It also detracts a bit from the main caveman-brain perks of the mutual fund: That it's both cheap and simple to buy into and usually generates returns with minimal fuss.

It's no surprise that the passive model is much more popular. Traditional IRA/RRSPs are still much more popular than Roth/TFSAs, but we've demonstrated how that popularity doesn't conflate to the wisest of investments. A passive mutual fund means our fund manager, the person we're trusting our money to, doesn't need to maintain much care or involvement other than making sure they have a bot or an app tracking how different stocks are performing in the market.

This tracking tends to be good, as it strictly sticks to what the math says will be the best outcome, but it's not as good at tracking changes that could alter the equation entirely. Our money is still vulnerable to market fluctuations. The lack of active involvement can also mean struggles to get consistent customer support when these fluctuations become worrying, as Stacy found to her detriment.

The average worker like Stacy has more urgent things to do than keeping eyes on a string of accounts while keeping up with market variations just to figure out why she's seeing losses in her fund. In her case, she was a single parent working long hours to provide for a child who requires additional time and care due to physical and learning disabilities. It's easy to burn ourselves out with incredible stress if we try to take on the fund manager's job in addition to balancing our work and family responsibilities.

I wouldn't recommend Roths/TFSAs if most of their investments ended up this way, but, for the sake of friends like Stacy, I must mention that, when deciding what to do with the money we put in those accounts, we have better options than passive mutual funds.

Even simple active mutual funds are much better in Roth IRAs. Active mutual funds tend to generate a lot more money in the short term but are traditionally held back by the higher tax. In a Roth IRA, they don't get taxed. We get to have our cake and eat it, too. But we can even do one better than that.

Segregated Funds & Active Accounts

Segregated Funds, or SFs, are a Canadian investment tool that is similar to a mutual fund in that we're paying money into a collected pool that is then managed by professionals.

However, it's also similar to the US Active-Managed Separate Account, or SA, as both of them are insurance-based investment funds. They also both require, by law, that the customer's invested assets be kept separate from the assets of the insurance company itself, hence the names "separate" or "segregated."

The service is offered by insurance companies but isn't used by them to fuel their policies. For this reason, we can be confident our money will stay in that pool, or else go towards an investment that will generate returns.

Note that the SA should not be confused with the Separately Managed Account, or SMA, which is what may even happen if you try to look up either of them on the Internet. As I mentioned earlier, the US variation of these accounts is less clearly defined, so it is imperative to talk directly with the insurance companies to know exactly what they can offer us.

Unlike the SA, the SMA requires a minimum investment of $100,000 and so isn't the best option for the average working-class investor. These SMAs are also so-named because, instead of our money going into a pool, it's just ours on its own. Quite a drastic difference, so we need to be careful when planning our investment. In some circles, the terms SA and SMA are used interchangeably even by industry professionals, so it can be even more confusing: Be sure to clearly define our fund before we attempt to invest in it.

From now on, the SA and SF will be referred to collectively as an SA/SF.

In some US regions, SA/SFs might even be completely unavailable. Traditional mutual funds are still just fine, but if we're worried we might wind up like Stacy from Chicago, there are still a few things we can try.

The first thing we can do is contact the relevant insurance companies directly, and ask them if they offer separate account options. If that doesn't work, we can be a little more creative and ask them if they'd instead be willing to create similar funds based on the Canadian model.

A good business loves to innovate when it smells opportunity. Just ask acclaimed US fund manager Michael Burry: If the financial service we need doesn't exist, ask if they'll create it for us. In his case, the innovation was credit default swap options which made him a billionaire after he accurately foresaw the inevitability of the 2007 Subprime Mortgage Crisis. If you don't know what I'm talking about, go watch *The Big Short*. After studying the crisis in greater detail, I suspect it overlooked a few key factors which contributed to the advent of the crisis, but it's still a great film that humorously breaks down complicated investment matters to an understandable level for an everyday viewing audience.

In any case, while it might seem daunting to request a service instated just for us, remember that, while most of us are learning our finances backward, the people running insurance companies, especially long-established ones, tend to know exactly what they're doing. They will be aware of how satisfied Canadian investors are with their segregated funds, which have superior protections compared to regular mutual funds, ultimately benefiting both the investor and the brokering insurance company.

Even in 2021, people are still going through the fresh trauma of the 2007 crisis, meaning consumers and creators are both looking for ways not only to grow their money but also to protect it in case another major upset occurs.

Before moving on, there are a few important things to note about the Canadian model:

1. A segregated fund is a contract. Always read a contract carefully before agreeing.
2. One of their terms will likely be a penalty if we withdraw too early. Know all specifics of minimum investment periods.
3. Even in an absolute worst-case scenario, such as the company being reduced to atoms, we'll still get back 75-100% of the money we put in due to legally mandated investment protections.
4. Since the service is often offered by insurance companies, many segregated funds come with a death benefit. If we pass away while our contract is still active, the money we put in will instead be given tax-free to the beneficiary of our choice.
5. Depending on our contract, we can keep our contributions protected from bankruptcy, insolvency, or even lawsuits. In difficult financial times, our funds cannot be seized. This is like having the benefits of a traditional IRA/RRSP through our Roth/TFSA. It's also one of the biggest upsides to this kind of fund, so

make sure our contract includes it! The peace of mind this offers can be incredible in hard times.

Now, as US economic policies and even tax rates can vary from state to state, I must once again urge that we get an advisor on board, particularly one who is well-versed in the way our state's economy works. Individual states can often be compared to countries due to their size and output. However, for segregated funds, we aren't necessarily looking for a general finance advisor, but rather for a life insurance agent who can be invaluable in any insurance-based investment fund.

Some financial service companies have even developed an entire model wherein life agents function as brokers, providing overarching insurance coverage and ideal investment opportunities, and it would be well worth your while to investigate which companies exist in your region. *World Financial Group* is one such company that operates in both the US and Canada, and has been showing very promising growth for several decades. However, the old mindset regarding these types of companies dies hard, and many of them will still be dismissed, even in online searches, as nothing more than a new variation on the Multi-Level Marketing scheme, or MLM. Do your research, and pay particular attention to verifiable long-term customer satisfaction. It's also important to note that few MLMs can last more than a very few years. Longevity is just as important for confirmation as happy customers.

There's a pervading stereotype that life agents are the modern-day door-to-door vacuum cleaner salesman. Much like insurance, vacuum cleaners are a great innovation, but the stigma attached to the most vigorous proponents of both products has been hard to shake off. Of course, if the agent who pitches to us turns out to be just a salesman who fast-talks and skims over their qualifications, then we should be prepared to refuse any offer until we have gotten every detail of the contracts and policies from someone who helps us feel confident in our decision, not just pressured into it.

I cannot overstate the difference that has been made in my own life by utilizing the services of fully qualified advisors and accredited life agents. I once even gave serious consideration to pursuing insurance brokering as a career, going so far as completing my licensing exams before deciding that other opportunities were better suited for me. However, the preceding course material alone was enough to open my eyes to countless opportunities which most people remain unaware of, and led me to continue researching obscure methods of investing which could change peoples' lives for the better. Doing the job of a life agent was not my final calling, but I never hesitate to refer anyone to those for whom it was.

Had I not considered a career as a life agent, I never would have written this book. The things I learned were that much of a wake-up call for my own life that I decided to continue developing strategies in a simple-to-understand format that could be shared with the world.

Insurance-based investing is still a relatively unknown and obscure area, which many people can readily admit to being confused by. In these situations, a qualified life agent can help us to look beyond our insurance company in the same way that a general finance advisor or mortgage broker would help us to look beyond our bank. For example, many of the financial companies who specialize in insurance-based investing train their life agents based on strong broker models developed by top-performing real estate companies.

The practical upshot of this is an astonishing impact on both savings and retirement plans, as strategies that might not be so viable before now have a chance to be the bee's knees. Having a great agent or advisor here is vital. Since SA/SFs are actively managed, they will, on average, have higher manager fees and, thus, slightly lower base returns compared to more passive funds, so the last thing we want is to settle for the first option we're given from a company that already offers these funds. Just like when looking for the best mortgage, the key is to find not just a strong company, but a reputable brokerage.

Likewise, for a company that doesn't yet offer these funds, the last thing we want is to try negotiating a better deal on our own. Just getting them to create the service already takes a bit of tact, and skewing the service away from favoring the parent company creating it would require even more.

A great broker or life agent will ensure we find an SA/SF comparable in returns to a good mutual fund, which will set us up for success as an individual before we even reach Step 6.

The Manager's Role in Active Accounts

While passive mutual fund managers are usually more than content to simply have an automated index reader to tick over, active managers are much more hands-on and much easier to speak to regularly. Just like it's a great idea to have a good agent or advisor, it's also a fantastic plan to find a good manager and to negotiate upfront around what their fees should be, as well as how often we'll be talking to them in non-emergency situations. The clearer the understanding before we start, the better our relationship with them will be going forward.

Historically, active investing only generates slightly better returns compared to any investment's passive counterpart but takes much more work. Since we have a manager on board, however, they're the ones who take on the work for us.

Although no one can truly see the future, their experience allows them to behave like our own personal tea-leaf reader. While a passive manager's virtual tools will be limited to the market's trends and indexes, the active manager is unconstrained in that sense, letting skilled managers perform above and beyond projected outcomes time and again.

Even the less skilled active managers, so long as they're at least competent, will have a much better ability at seeing sudden changes on the horizon compared to busy day-job investors such as ourselves and will be able to account for the irrationality of their fellow humans in ways a bot never will.

It can be quite risky working a nine-to-five job while also actively managing our growth investments. A manager makes this possible. This not only lets us enjoy the protection offered by the more actively managed SA/SFs, but the manager's vigilance will boost this protection even further through their actions.

For instance, a passive manager relies almost wholly on automated processes. The processes will then run according to projections and historical data. But what if the majority of our investments are now under threat, and these processes do not pick it up? An active manager, on the other hand, can swap our money between funds within our Roth/TFSA, giving us more protection through diversification by ensuring the majority of our money will always be in the safest place it can before an impending crisis hits.

Now, it's never fun to lose any amount of our investments. Stacy can attest to that. But imagine our money is split 20% and 80% between mutual funds and SA/SFs, a fairly common proportional split for investors. Let's say that we and all our friends are investing our 80% portions in mutual funds in the same market or industry. Theirs are passive, but ours are active.

How grateful would we feel if those portions we've invested take a huge nosedive in value, and we learn that our manager had already sold off and reinvested most of the money from the bad active funds into much better ones?

Even by swapping the 20% portion in a safe fund with the 80% which may be in a jeopardized fund, our losses will be greatly minimized: Whereas most people we know would've taken a severe hit to around 80% of their investment, we've only taken a hit to 20%.

A good active manager is like a form of investment insurance. It costs a little bit more to hire them, but they'll help to minimize our losses should something unexpected occur.

Questions to Ask Your Manager, Agent, and Advisor

When speaking to any of these three individuals, it always helps to ask the following questions, which I've numbered in no particular order of importance:

1. "I'm thinking of making X-dollars in contributions each month, and I want them to go first into my Roth/TFSA. Anything leftover can go into a traditional IRA/RRSP, or 401(k). What kind of investment markets should I look at for each account?"
2. "Within each of my accounts, how should the money I put in them be split by percentage between their constituent investments?"

3. "I want to achieve a comfortable retirement while maintaining a reasonable standard of living. With the time I have left, what should my risk tolerance be?"

4. "What level of risk does my current plan need, and is there a way to reduce it?"

Every investor is different, and managers, advisors, and agents help find the crucial balance needed for us to achieve enough growth for our goals while keeping risk at a comfortable level.

Something else worth noting is that many managers and advisors are just as traditional as most investors, i.e., they are not aware of the benefits outlined in this 6-step guide I've put together for you. That is another reason why life agents are more necessary than ever, as many of the strategies we've discussed are optimal for insurance-based investing which a life agent is far more likely to be familiar with. Your life agent is more likely to run like a Thoroughbred with these strategies, while an old-school advisor is more likely to balk like an old mule. It is again best for us to look for financial service companies specializing in insurance-based investing: They will be the ones who are most aware of the newer strategies because their entire company is based on them.

We've mentioned risk tolerance before, which is one more aspect that only our unique financial fingerprint can be used to identify. We all have different levels of risk that we are comfortable with.

To help gauge our comfort with risk, we can also ask ourselves questions like, "Do I feel the urge to check in on my investments every day?" If the answer is yes, then it's a sign that we get nervous over investing easily and would be better off emotionally with a lower-risk option.

Another self-reflection would be, "How much money am I willing to lose?" In other words, how many times would our contributions have to suffer massive losses in a row before money feels tight and we get cold feet about investing at all? The lower this number, the safer we'll have to play, as it's no good to push too hard and then lose out on such powerful growth because of a conditioned fear response.

Overall, it's good to know how nervous we are about investing before going in, as we'll have an easier time communicating our concerns to our agent when we meet. They can only personalize a plan for us if we give them *all* the information they need to do so successfully, and that includes information on an emotional level.

However, in the large majority of cases, we won't need to be particularly nervous at all. An active manager who we can actively correspond with is a fantastic extra layer of security for our Roth/TFSA, especially when it's put into a separate account, segregated fund, or active-managed mutual fund as we've discussed.

As trust is built between us and our manager, there's no reason they can't handle ETFs and Index funds for us as well, especially if done through our Roth/TFSA. In all cases, they render a valuable service that lets us live our own lives without keeping a constant eye on markets.

8

FILLING THE BUCKET BEFORE YOU KICK IT:

ADVANTAGES OF INVESTING IN A CASH-VALUE LIFE INSURANCE POLICY, AND OTHER INSURANCE PRODUCTS.

Insurance can be an important form of tax-sheltered cash to protect our savings and help out in times of crisis throughout our lives. When we have people to look out for, it's also good to make sure we have coverage on our life so that any extra savings we might have can be bequeathed to them in a will, rather than disappearing into a funeral.

Any extra earnings we have from our contributions at the end of life should ideally be allowed to continue growing, making things easier for the next generation of our family, and allowing life to continue improving in at least our small corner of the world.

Creating this buffer of insurance for our savings brings us to our final step.

Step 6: Invest in Cash-Value Insurance Products.

Way back in Chapter 3, we went over how mortgage life insurance is a bad idea, for reasons such as low chance of a payout, and the fact that the coverage goes to paying off one very specific kind of debt, rather than handing out cash to our loved ones for their free use once we're gone.

As a working person, there are two aspects of finance I deeply cherish. The one is a well-planned retirement and the other is knowing that my family will still be secure should something happen to me.

Steps 1-5 were all about us. At first glance, Step 6 would seem to be about what goes on in our immediate family's world after we're gone. However, that is not the case. Those types of insurance which carry a cash value can be of great value to us during our own lifetime, which is the primary reason I decided to include them in this book: They're just too dang beneficial at all stages to be overlooked as an investment tool.

What Kind of Insurance Should You Get?

Many of the options mentioned in Chapter 3 are good choices, but I'd like to briefly touch on a few more here.

Universal or Whole Life Insurance

This is the primary form of cash-value insurance, and is also one of the most popular forms, as we pay the same rate to keep it going each month. In return, we not only get a respectable-sized benefit for our beneficiaries, but we also build up cash in an investment portion, which grows tax-deferred interest. We are then able to make withdrawals from that cash-value while we're still alive, using it for whatever we wish.

The two primary types of cash-value policy are Whole Life Insurance and Universal Life Insurance, which are quite similar but with a couple of key differences.

With Whole Life Insurance, the investment portion offers annual dividends which can be used in a variety of ways: Cash payouts directly into our pockets, continued fund value and interest growth, reduced premium payments, or even increased coverage of the policy. Additionally, the cash-value is guaranteed: Should we choose to cancel the policy, we receive the accumulated fund value that we have contributed plus interest, although cancellation fees may apply. (For the sake of clarity, the cash payout to our beneficiaries is called a death benefit, while the portion of funds we can use in our lifetime is referred to as the policy's living benefits.)

Universal Life Insurance is also called adjustable insurance, as it can be altered by the policyholder as their circumstances dictate: The amount of the premiums paid can be changed as well as the payment schedule, and the death benefit can be increased or reduced. This flexibility is primarily what differentiates it from a Whole Life policy, and also what makes it a little riskier: If the investment fund is not generating sufficient growth or if the premiums are not kept at a maintainable rate, the policy may lapse. This is why an advisor or managing life agent is strongly recommended for those who choose this option, as they can monitor the fund value and select the best investments to keep the policy in good standing.

Because the available cash from either a Whole Life or Universal policy is technically an insurance payout, it doesn't get taxed while it's growing, making it yet another way to build wealth at a modest rate tax-free. However, generally, this cash-value is only loaned, meaning it's taken away from our coverage unless we pay it back.

As another personal example, my company was impacted by the COVID-19 pandemic just like the rest of the world and forced to institute temporary layoffs. For two months, I was out of work. Thanks to the investing I had done, this time without a paycheck was much easier to manage. During this time, I was able to use the built-up cash-value within my personal Universal Life Insurance policy—which I selected over the Whole Life Insurance option for a variety of reasons unique to my circumstances, as will be the case for any of us—to continue paying my premiums. Once I was back at work, I immediately paid the amount of those two premium payments back to replenish my fund's cash-value. This prevented the overall face value/death benefit of the policy from being impacted. By contrast, this was a far better scenario than that of many people who immediately canceled their insurance policies as soon as they got into a similar financial bind: Like Roth/TFSAs, insurance sadly tends to be viewed as an unnecessary luxury when we're suddenly worried about affording food and mortgage payments.

Overall, cash-value insurance is flexible in that we can effectively use part of it for all sorts of things while we're still alive and well, but the downside of this flexibility is the policies tend to be more expensive. On the other hand, the policy lasts for as long as we live, so long as we keep meeting our payments. This means, if we get a policy with conditions we like, we can look forward to enjoying those benefits for the rest of our lives, and don't have to worry about re-qualifying 10 or 20 years later when we are older and may be in poorer health, as is often the case if someone wants to renew a Term Life policy.

Note that life insurance doesn't get paid out automatically in most cases: Our beneficiary needs to know about it. They need to file a claim before receiving a payout, and they'll need a certified death certificate to do so. *Always* let your loved ones know the details of your life insurance provider. The provider can provide help in submitting insurance claims, taking the burden of confusion off our loved ones during an already difficult time.

Term Life Insurance

Another popular form of life insurance, this is also known as 'pure' life insurance. We can't take loans out of it as we can with cash-value insurance, but it is generally much cheaper. So, while not the best choice for building wealth or deferring taxes, it is still an affordable option that's good for our peace of mind. Note that Term Life Insurance only lasts for a certain amount of time, during which we must make our monthly payments.

When its time is up, we'll have to apply for term life insurance again if we still want it. Some people may decide that they no longer need it as they are older and may have fewer expenses, i.e., they may have taken out the insurance policy primarily for peace of mind while they were still making home and vehicle payments. If those debts have since been eliminated, and they have sufficient retirement savings which can be left to a beneficiary, the need for life insurance may have been rendered moot.

So, how is this different from just having a non-term policy that lasts forever so long as we keep up on our payments?

An insurance policy, or an insurance contract, generally cannot be changed while it's active. If we agree to a policy that lasts 20 years, the company can't change that policy's conditions. But, when it runs out and we have to get re-insured, the company is free to remove that policy type and offer a new version instead, with different costs or duration. For example, we may be ineligible for the same insurance coverage we had before due to changes in health, occupation, habits, and even our age.

Health Insurance

A bread-and-butter form of insurance for pretty much everyone in the US, health insurance will either pay our doctor or pharmacist directly, or it will reimburse us for what we paid. This insurance covers pretty much every medical, surgical, or prescription-related cost we can imagine. However, the coverage is only up to a certain preset amount, and usually only if we got our treatment from an associate of the insurance company.

This makes it good for consistent medical prescriptions and regular health checkups, potentially saving us a lot of money depending on where we live. Some health insurance policies even cover dental work.

The US has had a history of increasing taxes on those who don't have health insurance. This isn't the case at the time of this writing, but it's worth bearing in mind for those who hope to save their money in the future, in case those laws make a return. Again, we need to be aware of the intentions of our current government administration when planning our finances.

Disability Insurance

Disability insurance kicks in whenever an accident or sickness prevents us from working at our regular job. The amount we pay is between 1.5-3% of our gross income for the year, and the payout amount is about 45-65% of our gross income, tax-free. The policy intends to help tide us over while we have limited or no access to our regular income as a result of being debilitated for a long period. For this reason, the money will be paid to us in a monthly allowance until we get better, rather than as a lump sum for us to spend all at once.

We usually need to be older than 18 and younger than 60 to qualify for this coverage.

Because the company wants to be sure our disability is a long-term debilitation, they tend to have a very long waiting period before they payout. This is an unfortunate necessity for the insurance companies, as fraudulent claims in this area are some of the most prevalent forms of insurance fraud: It's a lot easier for a dishonest person to fake a back injury than it is to fake death or terminal cancer. This means we can't use disability insurance in place of normal health coverage or critical illness insurance. However, it is still a very wise investment. It gives us financial oxygen as we recover from a long-term injury or illness, and can give us the extra time we need to find new work if the disability is permanent.

Critical Illness Insurance

Critical illness insurance protects us from the financial costs incurred from the onset of cancer, heart attacks, strokes, and other similar health conditions. In the USA, the costs required for dealing with these critical illnesses can be far beyond what any normal health insurance plan is willing to cover.

They also tend to pay out directly in cash. This is because the initial estimated cost of our treatment is probably lower than what the actual cost will be, so the company would rather hand us what they promised and trust us to use it to pay off the costs as they mount.

This insurance form is surprisingly cheap, mostly because it only covers a very narrow array of medical issues. Always double-check insurance contracts to make sure the issues we want to be covered are actually covered. Most forms of critical illness insurance also cover some forms of surgery, like organ transplants and coronary bypasses, in addition to the conditions mentioned above.

The money can be used rather flexibly once paid out, but we still need to satisfy the above stipulations to receive it.

Estate Planning Insurance

Simply put, when a person moves on or is on the cusp of doing so, their family needs to make the difficult decision as to how to divide up their estate. This can be quite a complicated procedure, made even more difficult during times of grief, so a lawyer almost always has to be called in to help take stock of everything, as well as to carry out the will of the deceased as intended.

Estate planning insurance is a specialized form of life insurance that helps our will be enacted. Mortgages and owed taxes can be paid off by this insurance so that possessions that would normally have to be sold can instead be gifted to loved ones. This insurance can also be used to establish a support fund for a loved one, or even to make donations to a charity we support once we're gone, should we choose to make a charitable organization our beneficiary rather than a loved one or family member.

This is one of the most meaningful forms of insurance but is probably also the most commonly overlooked. However, the premiums are very reasonable, and it can be of invaluable assistance to a bereaved family.

All of the above insurance types are useful, but one, in particular, stands out for the purposes of this book...

Whole Life Insurance and Universal Life Insurance, aka Cash-Value Insurance

The flexibility of Whole Life and Universal Insurance, as well as their willingness to give us OPM through the form of temporarily withdrawing the money while we're still alive, has historically seen great use as a tax shelter for the wealthy, and some experts have even suggested without irony that this was the primary reason for which it was created.

This fact alone should make cash-value insurance a desirable option for the savvy everyday investor, as many others may erroneously still associate the policy with "rich people insurance," dismiss it, and then move on to a term life policy instead. They even feel financially validated in their decision, as term life premiums are generally lower. But the truth is, a cash-value policy with a death benefit into the high six-figures can be acquired with payments of only a couple hundred dollars a month. That is an easy amount for the average family to budget for, and the benefits for the whole family, in life and death, can be huge.

The money we put into our insurance policy's cash-value doesn't get taxed. At the time of this writing, it isn't usually taxed even after we withdraw it unless the withdrawal exceeds a certain amount, in which case it is counted as income again. This is what typically happens the moment we start withdrawing the interest our cash-value has accrued, so be careful.

Generally speaking, the longer we've held our insurance policy, the more we're able to safely withdraw. We can make these withdrawals at any time, for any reason, and the money can go to anything. As mentioned earlier, we don't even have to pay it all back so long as we're willing to accept a lower death benefit for our loved ones once we're gone. Since the death benefit is normally quite large as well as tax-free, this isn't usually a huge problem. Going back to my example, had I chosen to not pay back the two premiums which I allowed to be paid from out of the fund value during the two months when I was out of work, the total impact to my death benefit or fund value would have been less than $500. Not much of a hit when we're dealing with a payout in the hundreds of thousands or even millions of dollars.

Such a choice can also be well worth it for our loved ones, depending on what we're planning. For instance, these withdrawals could help us pay for Li'l Sue's education, or even invest in other forms of growth while still having peace of mind that our family will be okay should the worst happen. We can also use these withdrawals to supplement our retirement fund, allowing a more comfortable life. Finally, using the fund value for paying premiums is not just reserved for lean times such as my two months when I was not working, either. This strategy can also be used by retirees.

For example, elderly people who have paid for the upkeep of their policy over many years can likewise use this "recycling" of their cash withdrawals right back into their premium payments in exchange for a gradual reduction in their cash-value or death benefit. Particularly if they have sufficient other investments and retirement savings bequeathed to loved ones,—as mentioned earlier, investment tools such as Roth/TFSAs also offer tax-free payouts to a beneficiary—this is a great way for people in retirement to keep their policies active with virtually no out-of-pocket expense and very little long-term impact: The cash-value they can borrow against will be a considerable amount, as they have been building it up for decades, and they may never use up all of it in their lifetimes.

Under differing circumstances, we can instead invest the money we withdraw into our Roth/TFSA once we're retired, giving us another way to keep it growing even when we're technically no longer earning an income. This is one of the best ways to use the money from this life insurance policy even before we're retired, provided it allows us to contribute more to our best growth accounts than we otherwise could.

Some people in retirement even manage to continue payments to both their cash-value insurance policy *and* their Roth/TF-SAs... using only the withdrawals from their policy's cash-value! Since their growth accounts will have accrued substantially through ongoing compound interest by this time, the impact on their policy's face value is lessened even further.

Building on that, getting a cash-value insurance policy like this works very well when we're young: The younger we are, the lower our monthly rates for life insurance are, and, remember, our monthly rates don't change under this policy, unlike when we try to renew a term life insurance policy. Normally this wouldn't be a huge advantage, since lower rates don't mean much when we're paying them for longer, but the fact that we're building up usable cash-value at the same time makes this fantastic. Compound interest in our favor is just as sexy as ever, even through insurance.

Many advisors I've spoken to recommend that we let our cash-value build for at least 10 to 15 years before we try to withdraw it, to get a sizeable amount. So if we want to use it earlier, we need to start building it earlier.

If we don't want to make withdrawals from our life insurance directly, we could alternatively use the amount we've built up as a security promise when taking out loans elsewhere, which can be helpful when getting the equipment we need to start a new job, or even our own small business. We can also choose to take a loan from the insurance company itself, using our policy as security. Because we're essentially borrowing against our own money, the company typically offers much lower interest rates than banks do, making this kind of life insurance a way to access credit relatively cheaply.

Even with a relatively new cash-value policy with little built-up value, this can be an option: The loan simply becomes covered by a portion of our death benefit. Should we die before repaying the loan, the loan is automatically paid back to our creditor, and the remainder goes to our beneficiary.

In fact, some types of business loans require the applicant to take out a life insurance policy for the additional security of the lender. This is particularly true in cases of "key-man" insurance, wherein a business venture is largely or fully contingent on the survival of one person: No matter how delicious his secret brine-and-spice recipe may be, *Pop Gherkins' Pickle Emporium* may not thrive so well if Pop Gherkins himself isn't greeting the customers every day, or if he dies and leaves the business to a sulky nephew who won't even wear Pops' iconic straw boater hat. That's the kind of thing that business investors need to consider, which is one more reason to have a good insurance policy with usable cash-value in place well ahead of time, particularly if you have an entrepreneurial spirit.

In some cases,—although this can be more difficult—the death benefit of a life insurance policy can even be used as collateral for personal loans from a bank. Again, in the event of the policyholder's death before the repayment of the loan, the balance owing is repaid from the death benefit before the beneficiary receives the remainder. However, this often requires negotiating with our loan officer, and the bank will generally prefer that our policy's investment fund already have several years of built-up cash-value before agreeing to its use as loan collateral.

The only caveat I must give is to consult with an advisor before making sudden moves. It is recommended that we keep track of our insurance policies, as well as how much we can withdraw from a Whole Life, Universal, or other cash-value policy. If we are ever uncertain, ask our advisor.

Withdrawing too much too early can trigger penalties on top of the deferred tax that often comes with withdrawing our interest. Get too greedy, and we can even endanger our death benefit or render it useless, so we need to keep careful track of what we withdraw and how it impacts the remaining death benefit, similarly to how we would check the balance of any other account when we withdraw from it.

Recklessness is never a sound financial plan. Take care in our planning, and don't spend more than we need to. All of the positives listed above are just to let us know what's possible, and what strategies a cash-value insurance policy can help us fulfill.

Final Word

Insurance, when we personalize the policy to our unique needs, can be a wonderful source of relief in times of strife, debt, emergency, and death. Cash-value insurance is one of the most powerful ways to insure our death while still building some extra personal wealth on the side. However, this account isn't as core to our strategy as the Roth/TFSA. If one of those two accounts is mandatory for a comfortable life later on, cash-value insurance is more what I'd call 'recommended.' Strongly consider it, but make sure that we and our loved ones are getting more out of it than we're paying to keep it. And, now more than ever, make sure that the life agent we're working with has a strong track record of customer satisfaction.

No matter what insurance type we take out, its value ultimately comes down to how its policy is structured. There's a reason extremely wealthy people love to use cash-value insurance: It's a great financial tool that can "interact" well with our debts, payments, and other investments. However, if chosen poorly, or if we have no clear plan for using the cash-value to contribute to our other investments or a loved one's future, then we might be better off just using a regular term life policy.

CONCLUSION

All things being understood, we're now equipped to reevaluate the way we look at long-term prosperity. Life goes on, the world changes, and it pays to adapt to it. While many things are best left to full-time professionals, I hope that you've taken away enough from what I've shared to make some great decisions for your future and your family.

Remember the six steps.

Step One: Learn to look beyond your bank. All you need to do is put that learning into action. If you're perpetually frustrated paying off a mortgage, seek out a broker and get a better deal. If you can't find a growth account with a satisfying interest rate, call an advisor or life agent. It'll save a lot of agony later on.

Step Two: Embrace the concept of using Other Peoples' Money. Some debts need to be paid off quickly to avoid mounting interest. Other debts have such low-interest rates that it's better to focus on investing even before the debt is fully paid off. You've seen how powerful it can be to invest in financial growth early on. Whether you're in a mortgaged house or even just a long-derided rental property, you can have incredible long-term investment options attached to your home.

Step Three: Learn the Rule of 72. This is a hard and fast rule that'll help you tell at a glance if the growth account you're looking at will generate enough interest for the goals you wish to achieve. Don't forget the compound interest calculator from Chapter 5, either!

Step Four: Open your Roth IRA or TFSA first, especially if you live in the USA. You can only contribute so much to these accounts each year, but they can have great return rates, fewer traps down the road, creditor protections, no term limits or mandatory withdrawal dates, and can be easily left to a beneficiary as a tax-free payout. The sooner you open this account, the sooner you can capitalize on that positive while minimizing its negative. Also, strongly consider getting a Roth IRA for your child as soon as they begin any form of verifiable employment.

Step Five: Put some sort of actively managed or segregated fund into your Roth IRA or TFSA. It can cost a little more, but what you get is a more active and attentive manager, along with more protections, which can result in exponentially greater investment returns.

Step Six: Invest in cash-value insurance. This is a great way to not only open up another source of OPM but also to give yourself peace of mind. Your family is depending on you.

Put these steps into action, remember the caveats we've covered, and I'm confident you'll succeed.

If you enjoyed this book, the best "Thank you!" I can ask for is a detailed review and recommendation on Amazon or another online bookseller of your choice. For additional value and financial insights, you can subscribe for free to my website at www.paxtonsfinnegan.com. There, you will receive a free online copy of my in-depth guide, *The Law-Abiding Pirate*, to learn further strategies for maximizing your investments while protecting your money from the omnipresent ravages of inflation. That's just a couple of the ways that the Internet can truly benefit small businesses and freelance workers such as myself in our ever-changing technological landscape.

Finally, please consider this book to be your invitation to join our Facebook group, *You Can't Have My Money!* It's a great place to share financial ideas, tips, and discussions with a large community of everyday investors from around the world, as well as getting the inside scoop on my upcoming projects. We all have a thought no one else has thought of, and we all have something to share for the financial benefit of all. I look forward to chatting with you. (No, I don't farm out my Facebook obligations to some patsy.)

Happy trails, and don't let *anyone* undeserving have your money.

REFERENCES

Anspach, D. (2021, April 15). *9 things people don't know about Roth IRAs.* The Balance.

https://www.thebalance.com/surprising-roth-ira-facts-2388898

Banks Editorial Team. (2020, May 11). *Are there any tax-free savings accounts in the USA?* Banks.com.

https://www.banks.com/articles/banking/savings-accounts/tax-free-savings-accounts/

Bell, A. (2021, February 24). *6 ways to capture the cash value in life insurance.* Investopedia.

https://www.investopedia.com/articles/personal-finance/082114/6-ways-capture-cash-value-life-insurance.asp

Bieber, C. (2018, May 24). *Pay your mortgage early or invest?* The Motley Fool.

https://www.fool.com/mortgages/2018/05/24/pay-your-mortgage-early-or-invest.aspx

Bieber, C., Backman, M., & Brockman, K. (2021, March 6). *Retirement battle royale: 401(k) vs. IRA vs. Roth.* The Motley Fool.

https://www.fool.com/investing/2021/03/06/retirement-battle-royale-401k-vs-ira-vs-roth/

BravoPolicy. (2021, June 14). *Underfunded universal life insurance: Everything you need to know.* BravoPolicy.

https://bravopolicy.com/life-insurance/underfunded-universal-life-insurance/

Canada Revenue Agency. (2021, January 18). *Canadian income tax rates for individuals - current and previous years.* Canada.ca.

https://www.canada.ca/en/revenue-agency/services/tax/individuals/frequently-asked-questions-individuals/canadian-income-tax-rates-individuals-current-previous-years.html

Chase. (2021). *How to consolidate your credit card debt.* Chase.

https://www.chase.com/personal/credit-cards/education/basics/how-to-consolidate-your-credit-card-debt

Connett, W. (2020, October 20). *The best Roth IRA invest-ments.* Investopedia.

https://www.investopedia.com/articles/personal-finance/
110614/most-common-roth-ira-investments.asp

Dave, P. (2020, December 27). Whole Life vs. Universal Life Insurance. Investopedia. https://www.investopedia.com/articles/pf/07/whole_universal.asp

Eneriz, A. (2021, April 28). *Debt avalanche vs. debt snowball: What's the difference?* Investopedia.

https://www.investopedia.com/articles/personal-finance/
080716/debt-avalanche-vs-debt-snowball-which-best-you.asp

Hayes, A. (2020, October 3). *Mutual fund.* Investopedia.

https://www.investopedia.com/terms/m/mutualfund.asp

HowToSaveMoney Team. (2021, March 29). *Segregated funds Canada: The pros, cons, and alternatives.* HowToSave-Money.ca.

https://www.howtosavemoney.ca/segregated-funds

Investment Executive Staff. (2010, February 4). *91% of Cana-dians have retirement worries: Poll.* Investment Executive.

https://www.investmentexecutive.com/building-your-
business/financial-planning/91-of-canadians-have-retirement-
worries-poll/

Kagan, J. (2021a, April 30). *Complete guide to estate planning.* Investopedia.

https://www.investopedia.com/terms/e/estateplanning.asp

Kagan, J. (2021b, July 9). *Disability Income (DI) insurance.* Investopedia.

https://www.investopedia.com/terms/d/diinsurance.asp

Kilroy, A. (2020, May 20). *What to know about cash value life insurance.* Forbes Advisor.

https://www.forbes.com/advisor/life-insurance/cash-value-life-insurance/

Kumok, Z. (2021, June 28). *Critical illness insurance: What is it and who needs it?* Investopedia.

https://www.investopedia.com/articles/personal-finance/010416/critical-illness-insurance-who-needs-it.asp

Lanctot, P. (2019, December 12). *Insurance that will pay the mortgage if a spouse dies.* PocketSense.

https://pocketsense.com/insurance-pay-mortgage-spouse-dies-3255.html

McClelland, C. (2019, September 30). *More than a third of Canadians have no retirement savings, half live paycheque to paycheque, poll finds.* Financial Post. https://financialpost.com/personal-finance/more-than-a-third-of-canadians-have-no-retirement-savings-half-live-paycheque-to-paycheque-poll-finds

McWhinney, J. (2018, February 6). *A brief history of the mutual fund.* Investopedia.

https://www.investopedia.com/articles/mutualfund/05/mfhistory.asp

Ng, K. (2021, February 11). *TFSA investors: 1 top growth stock to buy and hold forever.* The Motley Fool Canada.

https://www.fool.ca/2021/02/11/tfsa-investors-1-top-growth-stock-to-buy-and-hold-forever/

Pant, P. (2020, July 13). *Actively vs. passively managed funds.* The Balance.

https://www.thebalance.com/actively-vs-passively-managed-funds-453773

Phung, A. (2020, March 7). *How do segregated funds differ from mutual funds?* Investopedia.

https://www.investopedia.com/ask/answers/06/segfundsvsmutualfunds.asp

Resendiz, J. (2021, January 28). *How credit card companies make and earn money.* ValuePenguin.

https://www.valuepenguin.com/how-do-credit-card-companies-make-money

Richmond, S. (2021, March 30). *Roth 401(k) vs. Roth IRA: What's the difference?* Investopedia.

https://www.investopedia.com/articles/personal-finance/063015/roth-401k-vs-roth-ira-one-better.asp

Rotter, K. (2021, March 30). *What to do after maxing out your 401(k) plan.* Investopedia.

https://www.investopedia.com/articles/personal-finance/070615/i-maxed-out-my-401k-now-what.asp

Sato, G. (2020, November 26). *Is it better to use a mortgage broker or bank?* Experian.

https://www.experian.com/blogs/ask-experian/is-it-better-to-use-a-mortgage-broker-or-bank/

The Investopedia Team. (2021a, January 10). Savings account vs. Roth IRA: Knowing the difference (E. Howard, Ed.). Investopedia.

https://www.investopedia.com/ask/answers/06/savingsvs.ira.asp

The Investopedia Team. (2021b, January 18). *Baby Boomer* (B. Barnier, Ed.).

Investopedia.

https://www.investopedia.com/terms/b/baby_boomer.asp

Thorp, B. (2021, April 20). *What are active ETFs?* Wealthtender.

https://wealthtender.com/insights/investing/etfs/actively-managed-etfs

U.S. Securities and Exchange Commission. (2021). *Compound interest calculator.* Investor.gov.

https://www.investor.gov/financial-tools-calculators/calculators/compound-interest-calculator

Wathen, J. (2017, October 5). 3 benefits of an actively managed fund. The Motley Fool;

https://www.fool.com/investing/2017/10/05/3-benefits-of-an-actively-managed-fund.aspx

Wilhoit, T. (2014, May 11). Accumulate wealth with the Rule of 72. YourFriend4Life.

https://www.yourfriend4life.com/accumulate-wealth-with-the-rule-of-72/